CREATING UNFORGETTAB

"In this book, Linda Seger takes us firmly by the hand and leads us down into the core of the drama, illuminating the lives of the people who live there, that they may teach us more about ourselves. A unique and absorbing work, it belongs on the 'Must Read' list of every serious writer."
> —Barry Morrow, writer, *Rain Man, Bill on His Own, The Karen Carpenter Story*

"Linda Seger has provided creative TV and film executives with a short course on how to work with a writer, honing and improving the script through the most important dynamic of all—character development. I don't know how we do our job to the utmost without Linda Seger."
> —Barbara Corday, former president Columbia Pictures Television, cocreator of "Cagney and Lacey"

"Here's a nuts and bolts approach to understanding and applying character to scripts. It asks the right questions that will stimulate the writer and is a valuable tool for creating memorable lives on film."
> —Jeremy Kagan, writer/producer/director, *The Chosen, The Journey of Natty Gan*

"Character development is the hardest part of writing a novel. Linda Seger's suggestions create a frame of mind which makes writers more sensitive about other people and gives them a new way of viewing people in their lives."
> —Robin Cook, novelist, *Coma, Mutation, Harmful Intent*

"This book is a valuable resource for creating those well-drawn characters that attract great actors."
> —Dianne Crittenden, casting director, *Witness, Black Rain, Star Wars*

ALSO BY LINDA SEGER

Making a Good Script Great

CREATING UNFORGETTABLE CHARACTERS

Linda Seger

AN OWL BOOK
HENRY HOLT AND COMPANY
NEW YORK

Copyright © 1990 by Linda Seger
All rights reserved, including the right to reproduce this
book or portions thereof in any form.
Published by Henry Holt and Company, Inc.,
115 West 18th Street, New York, New York 10011.
Published in Canada by Fitzhenry & Whiteside Limited,
91 Granton Drive, Richmond Hill, Ontario L4B 2N5.

Library of Congress Cataloging-in-Publication Data
Seger, Linda.
Creating unforgettable characters / Linda Seger. — 1st ed.
p.   cm.
"An Owl book."
1. Drama—Technique.   2. Characters and characteristics in
literature.   3. Motion picture plays—Technique.
4. Fiction—Technique.   I. Title.
PN1689.S44   1990   89-48877
808.2—dc20   CIP

ISBN 0-8050-1171-4 (pbk.)
Henry Holt books are available at special discounts
for bulk purchases for sales promotions, premiums,
fund-raising, or educational use. Special editions or
book excerpts can also be created to specification.
For details contact: Special Sales Director,
Henry Holt and Company, Inc., 115 West 18th Street,
New York, New York 10011.

Designed by Katy Riegel

Printed in the United States of America
Recognizing the importance of preserving the written word,
Henry Holt and Company, Inc., by policy, prints all of its
first editions on acid-free paper. ∞

7   9   11   13   12   10   8   6

GRATEFUL ACKNOWLEDGMENT
IS MADE TO THE
FOLLOWING FOR PERMISSION
TO USE THE MATERIAL INDICATED:

Warner Bros. Inc. for excerpts on pages 36–38, © 1989 Warner
Bros. Inc.; Paramount Pictures for excerpts from *Witness*, © 1985
Paramount Pictures Corporation; Castle Rock Entertainment for
excerpts from *When Harry Met Sally*, © 1989 Castle Rock Enter-
tainment; Faber and Faber Ltd. for excerpts from *Les Liaisons
Dangereuses* by Christopher Hampton, © 1985; Viking-Penguin for
excerpts from *Ordinary People* by Judith Guest, © 1979 by Viking
Press; United Artists Pictures, Inc. for excerpts from *Rain Man*,
© 1988 United Artists Pictures; Picturemaker Production Inc. and
Glenn Gordon Caron for excerpts from "Moonlighting," © 1985;
MCA Publishing Rights for excerpts from *Midnight Run*, © Universal Pictures, a division of Universal City Studios, Inc., courtesy
of MCA Publishing Rights, a division of MCA, Inc.; Embassy Television and Columbia Pictures Television for excerpts from the "It
Happened One Summer, Part II" episode of "Who's the Boss,"
written by Martin Cohan and Blake Hunter, © 1985 Embassy
Television; Paramount Pictures for excerpts from the "Showdown,
Part I" episode of "Cheers," written by Glen and Les Charles,
© 1990 by Paramount Pictures; Lorimar Television for excerpts
from the "Conversations with the Assassin" episode of "Midnight
Caller," written by Richard DiLello, © 1988 Lorimar Television;
Samuel French, Inc. for excerpts from *One Flew Over the Cuckoo's
Nest*, © Dale Wasserman; United Artists Corporation for excerpts
from *War Games*, © 1983 United Artists Corporation; 20th Century
Fox Film Corporation for excerpts from *Broadcast News*, a Gracie
Film, a 20th Century Fox Production, © 1988; Dramatists Play
Service for excerpts from *I Never Sang for My Father*, written by
Robert Anderson, © Robert Anderson; Random House for excerpts
from *Act One*, written by Moss Hart, © 1959 Random House,
New York.

DEDICATED TO MY FAMILY—

to my parents
Agnes and Linus Seger

and my sisters
Holly and Barbara

Acknowledgments

WITH MANY THANKS

TO
my editor, Cynthia Vartan,
who has worked with me on both of my books,
and whose insights and encouragement
provide an atmosphere for creativity to unfold;

TO
my agent, Martha Casselman,
for her hard work and clarity;

TO
my friend and colleague Dara Marks,
whose good advice, clear original perceptions,
and emotional support have been
so important to this process;

TO
Lenny Felder,
for the title, his professionalism,
and good ideas;

T O
Cathleen Loeser and David Oates,
whose brainstorming helped me think
through Chapters 4 and 8;

T O
readers (and screenwriters)
Lee Batchler and Janet Scott Batchler, Ralph Phillips,
Lindsay Smith, and Lynn Rosenberg,
for reading the book,
helping me test and clarify the concepts,
and giving many hours of their time
to help fine-tune the manuscript;

T O
Dr. Alan Koehn from the C. G. Jung Institute
for reading Chapter 4,
to playwright Paul Carter Harrison and Dianne Piastro
from the Media Access Office
for reading Chapter 10;

T O
Susan Raborn,
for research, hours of transcribing the tapes,
and being so readily available when
I needed her;

T O
the folks at Friendly Computer Store
in Santa Monica, for all their technical support;

A N D T O
my husband, Peter Hazen Le Var,
for listening to me think,
helping me brainstorm,
and always giving loving support.

Contents

CONTENTS

Preface

A number of years ago, I was called in by a television producer who was confronting a character problem in one of her scripts. A well-known, respected actor was already cast in the role, but the part was limited in its scope. During the consulting session, we brainstormed further emotional layering, other dimensions to his character, and potential transformations. Later, the actor was nominated for an Emmy for his performance.

Some months later, I was asked to consult with some producers of a series that was in trouble. Ratings were low, the network was threatening to cancel. Although the acting was excellent, and the broad strokes of the characters were well drawn, there was little character expansion. In an evening seminar, we brainstormed potential conflicts, story issues that could expand character dimensionality, dynamic relationships that were already part of the series but had been unexplored, and reasons why audiences might want to be involved with these characters week after week. The producers were enthused, and set about to turn the show around. But it was too late. The network had already decided to cancel. Since then, the multitalented and popular star has not yet found another series, in spite of a number of successes in the past.

In both these situations, character was the key to a workable story. Great characters are essential if you want to create great fiction. If the characters don't work, the story and theme will not be enough to involve audiences and readers. Think of the memorable characters in the novels of *Gone With the Wind, To Kill a Mockingbird, Jane Eyre, Tom Jones*; or from the plays *Amadeus, Les Liaisons Dangereuses, The Glass Menagerie*; the films *Casablanca, Annie Hall, Citizen Kane*; the television series "I Love Lucy," "All in the Family," "The Honey-mooners." Even action-adventure films such as *48 HRS., Lethal Weapon*, and *Die Hard*, and horror films such as *Nightmare on Elm Street* credit their success to strong, well-drawn characters.

Creating unforgettable characters is a process. Although some writers say that it can't be taught, as a script consultant I've learned that there are processes and concepts that can effectively improve characters. By talking to many critically acclaimed writers, I've learned techniques and methods that great writers use to create great characters.

I also know that the problems that writers confront are confronted as well by producers, directors, executives, and actors. These are the people who must define the character problem, ask the right questions, and point the way to workable solutions.

The concepts within this book relate to the creation of all fiction characters and are based on the principles I've discovered as a drama professor, a theatre director, and, for the last ten years, a script consultant. For this book, I've interviewed over thirty writers who have articulated and affirmed these concepts; these include novelists and writers for film, television, plays, and advertising. Since my business focuses on screenplays, most of the examples are from film and television. Most of the literary examples come from novels and plays that have been made into films, since either the film or the novel will probably be known to most readers. During my conversations with novelists, they affirmed that all the character concepts I've discussed in relation to film and television are also applicable to the novel.

Since my previous book, *Making a Good Script Great*, deals with character in relation to story and structure, I have chosen not to repeat that information. Instead I will concentrate on the process of creating well-rounded individual characters, and characters in relationship. If you are a new writer, understanding these processes can help you know where to turn when inspiration seems to fail. If you're an experienced writer, you may have occasionally found that one of your characters just doesn't work. Reviewing these processes can help you understand what you do instinctively.

Character is created through a combination of knowledge and imagination. This book is designed to stimulate your creative process, and to take you through a process that will culminate in strong, dimensional, unforgettable characters.

CREATING UNFORGETTABLE CHARACTERS

1

~~~

Researching the Character

Some time ago, one of my writing clients came to me with a terrific concept for a script. She had worked and reworked the script for over a year. Her agent was excited and eagerly awaiting this new story.

Although she had been told that some of her scripts weren't strong enough for the American commercial market, this one was exciting and tough. It was the kind of story that many producers called "high concept"—with a strong hook and unique approach to the story, a clear conflict and identifiable characters.

Her first film had just been completed, and she was counting on this script to break new ground. She had to finish quickly—but the characters weren't working. She was absolutely stuck.

When I analyzed the script, I realized that she didn't know enough about the context—about the world of the characters. A number of scenes took place in a center for the homeless. Although she had spent some time serving soup at the center, and talking to the homeless, she had never experienced sleeping there or being on the streets. As a result, details and emotions were missing. It was clear that there was only one way that she could break through the character problems—she had to return to research.

The first step in the creation of any character is research. Since most writing is a personal exploration into new territory, it demands some research to make sure that the character and context make sense and ring true.

Many writers love the research process. They describe it as an adventure, an exploration, an opportunity to learn about different worlds and different people. They love seeing characters come to life after spending several days learning more about their world. When their research proves something they intuitively knew, they're overjoyed. Every new insight gained through research makes them feel they have made giant strides in creating an exciting character.

Others find research intimidating, and the most difficult part of the job. Many writers resist it, and resent spending hours making phone calls or foraging for information in the library. Research can be frustrating and time-consuming. You can go down a great many blind alleys before you accomplish a thing. You may not know how to begin to research a specific character point. But research is the first step in the process of creating a character.

The depth of a character has been compared to an iceberg. The audience or reader only sees the tip of the writer's work—perhaps only 10 percent of everything the writer knows about the character. The writer needs to trust that all this work deepens the character, even if much of this information never appears directly in the script.

When do you need to research? Consider for a moment: You're writing a novel. Everyone who has read it agrees that your protagonist, a thirty-seven-year-old white male, has a fascinating personality, but there are certain motivations they don't understand. You decide you need to learn more about the inner workings of your character. A friend suggests you read *Seasons of a Man's Life* by Daniel Levinson, about the male mid-life crisis. You also arrange to sit in on a group of men in analysis. Through this research, you hope to learn what happens to men in the mid-life transition, and how it motivates their behavior.

Or, you've just finished your script, but the supporting character of the black lawyer doesn't seem as fleshed out as the others. You contact the NAACP to see if they know a black lawyer who might be willing to talk to you. You need to gain an insight into ways the ethnic background will affect this particular character in this particular occupation.

Or, you've been assigned to write a film about Lewis and Clark. You're smart—you ask the studio for research money, transportation expenses, and eight months' time. You know you will need to understand the experience of the journey, and how the period will affect the characters and the dialogue.

GENERAL VS. SPECIFIC RESEARCH

Where to start? First, understand that you're never starting from scratch. You have been doing research your whole life, so there is a great deal of material to draw upon.

You are doing what's called *general research* all the time. It's the observation—the noticing—that becomes the basis of character. You're probably a natural people-watcher. You observe how people walk, what they do, what they wear, the rhythms of their speech, even their thought patterns.

If you have another profession besides writing—perhaps medicine, or real estate, or teaching history—all the material you absorb within those jobs can be applied when you write a script for a doctor series, or a story about the real estate profession, or a novel or screenplay that takes place in medieval England.

You're doing general research when you take classes in psychology, art, or science. Later, what you learned may give you the details you need for your next story.

Many writing teachers say, "Write what you know about"—and for good reason. They recognize that this constant lifelong observation and general research yields many details that might take months or years to learn if you were writing about an area outside your experience.

Carl Sautter, writer, former story editor of "Moonlighting," and author of *How to Sell Your Screenplay*, recounts the story of a writer who pitched a Fort Lauderdale story to him. "He wanted to do a film about four girls who go to Fort Lauderdale for spring break. It's an all-right idea, but I discovered that he had never been to Fort Lauderdale during spring break. We continued to talk and I discovered he came from a little farm in Kansas. And then he said, 'It's a shame I'm not there this week because this is pancake week.' This little town was having their annual pancake festival. And he starting describing all the things they do with pancakes, and all the details about the festival. And I said, 'Now there's a story. There's a wonderful setting for a movie.' And I said, 'Why take a story that two thousand people could write better than you can, about a situation you've never experienced? Write about something you know.'"

The creation of character begins with what you already know. But general research may not yield enough information. You'll also need to do specific research to fill in character details that may not be part of your own observation and experience.

Novelist Robin Cook (*Coma, Mutation, Outbreak*, etc.) is an M.D., but he still has to do specific research for his medical fiction books. "Most of the research is reading," he says, "but I do talk to doctors who specialize in the subject of my novel. In fact, I normally will work in that particular field for a few weeks. When I wrote the book *Brain*, which deals with a neuroradiologist, I spent two or three weeks with a neuroradiologist. For *Outbreak*, which was about a modern-day plague, I talked to the people at the Center for Disease Control in Atlanta, and researched viruses. For *Mutation*, I researched the science of genetic engineering. The pace of change in that field is so rapid that most of what I had learned in medical school was no longer valid. I put out a book a year. I usually spend six months of research, two months of generating the outline, two months writing the book, and a couple of months doing other things such as publicity and working at the hospital."

THE CONTEXT

Characters don't exist in a vacuum. They're a product of their environment. A character from seventeenth-century France is different from one from Texas in 1980. A character who practices medicine in a small town in Illinois is different from someone who's the pathologist at Boston General Hospital. Someone who grows up poor on an Iowa farm will be different from one who grows up rich in Charleston, South Carolina. A black, or Hispanic, or Irish-American will be different from a Swede from St. Paul. Understanding a character begins with understanding the context that surrounds the character.

What is context? Syd Field, in his book *Screenplay*, gives an excellent definition. He compares context to an empty coffee cup. The cup is the context. It's the space surrounding the character, which is then filled with the specifics of the story and characters.[1] The contexts that most influence character include the culture, historical period, location, and occupation.

CULTURAL INFLUENCES

All characters have ethnic backgrounds. If you're a third-generation American of Swedish-German background (as I am), the influence of this background may be minimal. If you're a first-generation black Jamaican, the ethnic background could determine behavior, attitudes, emotional expressiveness, and philosophy.

All characters have a social background. It makes a difference whether someone comes from a middle-class farming family in Iowa or an upper-class family in San Francisco.

All characters have a religious background. Are they nominal Catholic, Orthodox Jew, followers of New Age philosophies, or agnostic?

All characters have educational backgrounds. The number of years of schooling, as well as the specific field of study, will change a character's makeup.

All of these cultural aspects will have wide-ranging influence upon the makeup of the characters, determining the way they think and talk, their values, concerns, and emotional life.

John Patrick Shanley (*Moonstruck*) came from an Irish-American home, but observed his Italian neighbors across the street. He says, "I saw that they had better food. They were more connected to their bodies. When they spoke, they spoke with their whole selves. There were things about the Irish that I liked, too. They could, for example, outtalk the Italians. And they had a different brand of charm. So I took the best of both . . . for my writing and for my life."[2]

William Kelley researched *Witness* for about seven years, studying the Amish culture and trying to find a way to get more information from people who were not interested in talking to the public. "The Amish were very distrustful of Hollywood so I really had a terrible time breaking through until I met Bishop Miller—a buggymaker—and happened to mention to him that we would need about fifteen buggies to do this movie. Miller built buggies and being a good businessman he immediately said 'Uh-huh' and I suddenly had an entrée into viewing the Amish life."

Bishop Miller became the prototype for Eli in *Witness*. Through this association, Kelley learned that the Amish were bawdy, that they were "a good judge of horseflesh," that they had a good sense of humor, and that the women could be coy and flirtatious.

Culture determines speech rhythms, grammar, and vocabulary. Read out loud the dialogue that follows, to hear the voice of the characters.

In *Crossing Delancey*, by Susan Sandler, the Upper West Side language contrasts with that of the Lower East Side. In this case, all of the characters (except the poet) have a Jewish context, and come from a particular location in New York. Both of these contexts influence their speech.

Upper West Side Izzy describes her situation: "I met someone. It was an arranged meeting with a marriage broker. Grandmother set it up."

Bubba, the grandmother, speaks with another rhythm: "You want to catch the wild monkey, you have to climb the tree. A dog should live alone, not people."

Sam, the pickleman, from the Lower East Side, has a different style of speech: "I'm a pretty happy fella. I like to get up in the morning, hear the birds tweet tweet. I put on a clean shirt, walk to shul, make the morning prayers. Nine o'clock my doors open."

And the poet says, "You do have an exquisite stillness, Izzy."

Listen to the rhythms from the Irish play *Riders to the Sea*, by John Millington Synge: "They're all together this time, and the end is come. May the Almighty God have mercy on Bartley's soul, and on Michael's soul, and on the souls of Sheamus and Patch, and Stephen Shawn; and may He have mercy on my soul, Nora, and on the soul of everyone is left living in the world."

Listen to the difference in language between Eli, the Amish man, and John Book, the Philadelphia policeman. These rhythms are very subtle, but if you read the dialogue out loud, you'll hear the difference between the slight lilt in Eli's speech and John's directness.

ELI: You be careful out there among the English.

JOHN BOOK: Samuel, I'm a police officer. My job is to investigate this murder.

Many times, your stories will have characters from several different cultures. For those from your own culture, you can turn to your own experience to find the rhythms and attitudes. For characters from other cultures, you may need extra research to make sure that their cultures ring true, and to be sure that you've created separate characters—not simply characters with different names who all sound and act the same.

THE HISTORICAL PERIOD

It is particularly difficult to set a story in another period. Generally the research is indirect. A writer can't get direct information from walking the streets of twentieth-century London when the story takes place in the sixteenth century. Listening to the speech of the modern Englishman sheds only a bit of light on the speech that existed four hundred years before. The vocabulary is different, the rhythms are different, and even the words are different since many words and meanings have become obsolete.

Novelist Leonard Tourney, a history professor at the University of California in Santa Barbara, has written several books about sixteenth-century England, including *Old Saxon Blood* and *The Players' Boy Is Dead*. His professional background provides him with a knowledge of the period, yet he still has to research specific details when writing his books.

Leonard says, "I might need to know about the Inns of Court and its history and practices during the late sixteenth or early seventeenth century. One of my novels dealt with a witch trial. I had to learn whether a defendant would have been represented by counsel in the early seventeenth century. The answer was no—which makes the trial look strange. I had to learn how many judges sat on the panel, and whether there would have been a jury, and how many jury persons would have served. I had a kind of license based upon what I had learned that any kind of suspicious behavior at this time would have been adequate evidence to convict a suspect of witchcraft. I had to learn what punishment was meted out to witches."

Recently I consulted on a project about the Mormon trek west to Salt Lake City in the mid-nineteenth century. Kieth Merrill, writer and director, supplied the research information about historical speeches and details of the journey. Writer Victoria Westermark, who has written a number of scripts set in the nineteenth century, did a rewrite and polish. She explains how she was able to build upon past experience when determining characteristics and period language for the script, *Legacy.*

"Usually I pore over diaries, original letters, speeches the person might have made, if available. Although the written word is different from the spoken word, people reveal themselves through diaries. Letters can be very stiff. For another approach to the time, I read the local late-nineteenth-century newspaper, where I found the rhythms of the general public, their adamant likes and dislikes, and even the swearing.

"I've also researched at the Huntington library in Pasadena, where I was able to read original diaries. I keep lists by decade of interesting words or phrases that aren't in common usage but that add flavor and don't throw an audience by sounding too dated."

Even after copious research, you will often need to imagine details that you can't find, using everything you have learned so that the period will ring true.

LOCATION

Many writers set their stories in familiar locations. If you grew up in New York, many of your stories may take place there. Hollywood has thousands of scripts about people coming to make it in Hollywood. Or writers set scripts in places they've visited or lived in for short periods of time. The more knowledgeable someone is about the location, the less research is necessary. However, writers who know the area often find they need to return for specific research.

William Kelley had lived in the Lancaster County area of Pennsylvania. He already had a good start on location research for *Witness*. However, he still returned to the area to look for models for his characters, and to expand his knowledge of the Amish for this specific project.

James Dearden, writer of *Fatal Attraction*, is British, but he's spent considerable time in New York City—the setting for his film.

Two of Ian Fleming's James Bond novels, *Dr. No* and *Live and Let Die*, and several of his short stories were set in Jamaica, where he maintained an estate, Goldeneye. He visited Tokyo before writing *You Only Live Twice*, and wrote *From Russia with Love* after riding the Orient Express.

Location affects many different aspects of a character. The frenetic rhythm of Philadelphia in *Witness* is different from the slower-paced life on the Amish farm. The rhythm of the West in *Electric Horseman* is different from the rhythms of New York in *Working Girl*. And each will have an effect on the characters.

If you were writing the story "Rain," by Somerset Maugham (later made into two films), or *Night of the Iguana*, by Tennessee Williams, or *The Power and the Glory*, by Graham Greene, you would want to capture in your characterizations the sense of oppression from the heat and humidity, or the claustrophobic feeling that can come from the constant rain in the tropics.

If you were writing a book such as *In God We Trust*, by Jean Shepherd, or the script for *Never Cry Wolf*, by Curtis Hanson, Sam Hamm, and Richard Kletter, you would want to know how subfreezing temperatures can affect life-style and behavior.

Dale Wasserman, writer of the play based on Ken Kesey's novel *One Flew Over the Cuckoo's Nest*, had to do location research to understand his characters. "As part of my research, I went to asylums. I went to classy asylums and dreadful asylums. And then I arranged with the psychiatrist in a very large asylum to have myself committed as a patient for a time. Originally I was going to stay for three weeks but ended up staying for ten days. Not because it was scary or uncomfortable, but because of the opposite. It's extremely comfortable. I learned a few things I hadn't expected. Number one: that if you hand over your will and your volition to an institution life becomes very simple and the temptation to just keep on living it in just that way is very strong. I learned about the great range of patients, the articulateness, the various abilities."

When Kurt Luedtke wrote the screenplay for *Out of Africa*, he needed to know all about Karen Blixen's world in Africa in the 1920s and 1930s.

"As a boy, I was interested in Africa, so I'm sure I can look at my bookshelves now and find at least fifty books on East Africa. My research had taught me about the African frontier, that it hadn't even opened in 1892, that people lived on the edge of the known world."

His books supplied his general research, but Kurt had to do a great deal of specific research, too, to answer the questions that surfaced as he wrote the script.

"I needed to learn how coffee grows, and how it flowers, and how a plantation operates. I learned that by interviewing a coffee grower.

"I needed to have some understanding of what the relationships were between the whites, primarily Brits, and the Kenyan blacks. I needed to understand the African tribes, because Blixen is probably not using Kikuyu for the household servants, she's probably using Somalies.

"I needed to know that many white men were making a living through ivory hunting during this period.

"I needed to know about the government situation: was it a colony or was it a protectorate, who had the authority to do what, and what was the relationship between the government and the settlers?

"I needed to know the history of World War One in East

Africa. You don't normally think of World War One as having any effect in Africa, but the fact was, it did."

All of the many details—the slow pace of life where long stories are part of the evening's entertainment, the behavior between the colonists and the natives, the free-roving wild animals, and the economic instability of life on a coffee plantation—exemplified the considerable location research that helped make these characters work.

THE IMPACT OF OCCUPATION

Sometimes the context is the character's occupation.

Someone on Wall Street has a different pace and life-style from a farmer in Iowa. A computer analyst has different skills from an Olympic runner. A gardener and a podiatrist might have different attitudes, different values, different concerns as a result of their work.

James Brooks was attracted to the idea of *Broadcast News* because he was a real news buff. He had also spent some time in network news, but even with that background he still needed to devote about a year and a half to researching the script. As part of this research, he spent considerable time talking to newscasters and being an observer at news stations.

"I cared about the subject," he says, "and I'd say the first few months of the research were to get rid of my caring so that I could be as objective as possible and unlearn what I thought I knew.

"I started my research by talking to a lot of women— starting specifically with two, a Wall Street woman and a reporter. I was interested in the women who had made a mark, very fast, right out of college, well educated, top school, something good happened professionally right away.

"In some ways, the questions I asked were no different from the questions you would ask at various stages of a relationship, but it just felt more clinical."

Besides talking to people, James Brooks read up on the field. "I read the long biography on Murrow, I read some essays on news and broadcast, and whenever I'd hear about anything interesting, I'd track it down.

"I spent a lot of time in the city, hanging out with the people at the workplace. And if you spend enough time researching, your chances of being in the right place at the right time are enhanced."

By simply "hanging around," James Brooks saw many details that were incorporated into the film. "I saw someone run—physically run—when something went wrong with a tape."

I asked Kurt Luedtke how he would go about researching a certain character, for example, a safecracker. Since Kurt was once a journalist, he's very comfortable with the research process. He explained the process he would use to gain both character and story information.

"If I were doing a story about a safecracker, the first place I would go would be to the law authorities. I might ask, 'You haven't put anybody away lately who's literate and has half a brain and would be willing to talk to me?' Now one time in five or six somebody might say, 'Yeah, there's a guy who might be willing to talk to you, probably want to be paid, but if you give him a couple hundred bucks, he might be willing to talk to you.'

"Now I'm not necessarily looking for character information, but for vocational information, scene information. I'm surely going to ask him about the five times that a boost went wrong, what happened, just for the funny stories of how things go wrong. I'm probably looking for everything other than information about what the specific character would be because the guy in jail probably is not going to be useful to me. He's probably a true felon, while I'm probably writing about a less true felon for commercial reasons, in order to make my character more sympathetic."

Some of the questions that Luedtke would ask include:

"How does he pick his places? Who does he work for? If he works alone, why? What are the problems? Why did he pick safecracking rather than any number of other ways to get money? Where did he learn to crack a safe? What did he do as a kid?"

By asking these Who, What, Where, When, Why type of questions, Luedtke would begin to form some conclusions about what kind of person becomes a safecracker, and how he differs from other people who commit crimes. "I assume that out of the nature of safecracking goes a certain resistance to authority, a certain conservative approach to crime, as opposed to murder, or to robbery where you have to hold the gun on someone and think they might have a gun too. Safecracking is kind of a nice quiet job. You don't run into anyone else and your goal is mainly an economic one. You're not really a sociopath, you're just someone who lives outside the rules. You merely want the money."

Kurt would also listen for specifics of vocabulary. What are the current words that safecrackers use? This can't be found in the library. "A book that's been published in the 1970s might have some words, but it's probably an outdated vocabulary."

Kurt would then draw other conclusions from this information. "If he's careful, he's probably not a showboat; he does not want to be remembered, he is not going to be a flashy dresser. He probably doesn't do heists in the town in which he lives, but he flies into St. Louis to do his job and then gets out. . . ."

By thinking through what he's learned, Kurt begins to think of specific story points that would fit this character: "Because I know he's a careful person, he probably doesn't trust a lot of people. I know that probably a story mistake he's going to make is that he's been warned not to get so involved with people, and he probably gets involved with someone, which leads him into all sorts of trouble."

Through this type of interview, the writer begins to get basic information that rounds out the context and makes the character more realistic. This in turn can stimulate the creative process, helping the story emerge naturally and truthfully.

EXERCISE: If you were interviewing this safecracker, what other questions might you ask? About family? Life-style? Psychology? Motivations? Goals? Values?

CREATING SPECIFIC RESEARCH OUT OF GENERAL RESEARCH

Sometimes general research leads writers actually to model a character on someone they met.

When William Kelley researched *Witness,* he met models for both Eli and for Rachel. He says, "Bishop Miller himself became a character; he became Eli (although I'd never tell him this). I study character first by carefully looking at the face—the face is the map of the soul—and by listening very carefully to intonations and accents and merriment and if he's putting me on to see if I can tell. I wasn't allowed to take a picture of him so I memorized him.

"The model for Rachel came from Bishop Miller's daughter-in-law, who came out of the house one day. She was sort of coquettish, with a specific tilt of the head, a rather coy glance, and she said, 'So you're going to do a movie, am I going to be in your movie?' I said, 'Well, if you keep talking to me I can almost assure you, you will.' She was very pretty, she looked like Ali McGraw and was easy to pay attention to, about twenty-seven or twenty-eight."

For *Broadcast News,* James Brooks built the character of Jane as a composite of four or five women. Tom was based on a network correspondent he had heard about. "One person told me a story about what happened when this man was asked to go to Lebanon on an assignment. He said, 'No way; I'd quit first. I'm married and I have a kid. I'm not going to risk my neck in

Lebanon.'" Brooks recognized that here was an interesting character because he was going against the stereotype. In network news, most people would risk everything to get to Lebanon, but this man placed his wife and children first.

If you find a model for your character as a result of research, that's a plus. But the specific character need not come out of the research. That can come out of your imagination, provided you first understand the character's context.

SPECIFIC RESEARCH TIPS

In all of these discussions, a certain process is evident. Each of these people knew where to look and what to ask.

Asking the right questions is a skill that can be learned. Gayle Stone, writer of technical thrillers (*A Common Enemy, Radio Man*), is also a writing teacher. She says, "There are some people who go through life missing 90 percent of what is going on around them. Everyone has the capacity to pay attention. Some people can pay attention more easily, maybe because they got encouragement from their parents. Those people will have more information in their memory banks. If somebody can open the door for you and start to reveal that you're one of those people who really hasn't been paying attention, then the possibility is there—no reason why you can't start now. There is no time limit to observing life. As long as you're living and breathing you can do it, and you might be surprised at how much you actually know, how much your unconscious has been storing all along."

Many people are willing, even honored, to be asked questions about their work. Whether it means interviewing an FBI agent, talking to a psychologist who specializes in clients with obsessive behavior, or asking a carpenter to explain the names and uses of various tools—Who, What, Where, When, and Why questions will usually yield the necessary information.

"Get to know your librarian" is also valuable advice for any writer who needs fast access to information. Librarians will either know the answer or have ideas about where to find it.

HOW LONG DOES IT TAKE?

Research can take longer than any other part of scriptwriting. The length of time needed depends on what you know before you begin, and on the difficulties inherent in the character and the story.

James Brooks: "Research never stops. *Broadcast News* took a year and a half of absolute research and four years all together, because the research continued throughout the filming."

William Kelley: "I researched the Amish for seven years, and Earl and I wrote the script during the 1980 writers' strike, which lasted about three months."

Dale Wasserman: "*One Flew Over the Cuckoo's Nest* took three months to research, but I began with a very interesting book. And I took six weeks to write it."

Without adequate research, the writing process often takes longer, and can be filled with frustrations. Although research usually continues throughout the writing process, there are points when you know that you are familiar enough with a certain subject. James Brooks says you reach that point when "every additional person tends to confirm what you've already learned, and when you can be a full participant in shop talk among people in the area you're exploring."

A CASE STUDY:
GORILLAS IN THE MIST

In February 1989, Anna Hamilton Phelan was nominated for an Academy Award for Best Screenplay Adaptation for *Gorillas in the Mist*. This case study exemplifies a variety of ways that research can be used to create a character, even if, as in this instance, a character is based on a real person.

"I started researching Dian Fossey's character in mid-January 1986, just a few weeks after Dian was murdered. I finished researching on June first, started writing the screenplay on July first, and delivered it on September first. It took about five months to research, and eight weeks to write. It was so fast because I had everything there. I was so secure in what I had that it didn't take any time at all to put it down onto paper.

"I had to do different types of research for this story. The primatology information I needed to know I learned from books. I read everything that I could read about the mountain gorilla—all the back issues of *National Geographic,* anything that I could find in the UCLA library on the mountain gorillas of Ruanda. I learned about their night-nests, which became a scene in the film. I learned that a person should not make direct eye contact with the gorilla because that threatens them and will entice them to charge.

"I learned about the gorillas' protectiveness toward their families or their groups. There will be one gorilla—a juvenile male—who will guard the rest of the group. This worked very well because Digit, who was a juvenile male, was Dian Fossey's favorite gorilla. He was the one in the film who eventually put his hands in hers.

"During my time in Africa, I was looking for the smell, the feel, what the environment does to me visually. Although you certainly don't smell a character or an environment in a screenplay, you can get it there in between the lines. And I was looking for a sense of how dangerous the area was to live in. Much of the danger came from the discomfort of living ten thousand feet above sea level. Dian had emphysema, which was exacerbated by the climate. Smoking two packs of cigarettes a day plus living in that humidity made her emphysema much worse. The walking, the hiking, the schlepping up those mountains and sliding around in that mud made me ask, 'What kind of a woman would want to live in that kind of environment for fifteen years?' It's a long time to live in the mud and it's freezing cold. Absolutely bone-chilling cold. The coldest I've ever been in my life. It's so damp and you're always wet. There is no part of your clothing, when you're outside, that is ever dry.

"I stayed in a little cabin about fifty feet from the cabin in which Dian was murdered, because we were not allowed in her cabin. It had been cordoned off after the murder. However, I could look in the windows of the cabin. I wanted to get in to touch things. Sometimes in touching things that in this case real live people have touched—there is something that happens. And it's not even—I can't even express it—but there are certain feelings that you get that you can use in the work. And I knew, if I'd have been able to get in there and touch some things that she had touched, it would have probably been good for me. But I was able to look in the windows and see what it looked like inside this corrugated tin cabin where there were little tablecloths, little vases of dried flowers, little silver picture frames, good china, good silver. It was so bizarre, to see these valuables in this strange place, but that was what intrigued me about this woman.

"The first time I saw the gorillas, I thought, They're not real. They're so gentle and so docile and just kind of minding their own business that you're not frightened at all. But I never had that feeling about the gorillas that I know Dian had—that feeling of awe and wonder. So I had to create that feeling. But it was helpful for me to see the gorillas.

"The actual period of the story was more difficult to research, because the civil war which had formed a strong subplot in the story had been over with for a number of years. I did, however, find some information from Dian Fossey's book, where she mentioned a tiny bit in one of the chapters about her run-in at the border. There were other books I read, other historical accounts of the conflict in the Congo.

"The local people were very in awe and very much in love with Dian Fossey and/or her project. Those that had never met her were very taken with her. She was called Niramachebelli, and that means 'the woman who lives alone in the forest without a man.' But the people that I met that knew her better didn't like her. I only found one person out of the forty that I interviewed that liked her and that was Ross Car [played by Julie Harris in the film]. She had so many enemies. You could point your finger anywhere and find a murderer."

APPLICATION

As you think through your research, ask the following questions about your characters:

- What do I need to know about the context of my characters?
- Do I understand their culture?
- Do I understand the rhythms, the beliefs, the attitudes that are part of that culture?
- Have I met, talked to, and spent time with people in that culture?
- Do I understand ways that they are similar to, and different from the way I am?
- Have I spent enough time with a number of different people, so that I won't create a stereotype based on one or two encounters?
- Am I familiar with the occupation of my characters?
- Do I have a feel for the occupation, some sense through observation of what the work entails, and how people feel about their work?
- Do I know the vocabulary well enough that I can use it naturally and comfortably in dialogue?
- Do I know where my characters live? Do I know the lay of the land, the experience of walking the streets?
- Do I have a sense of the climate, of leisure-time activities, of the sounds and smells of this location?

- Do I understand how this location is different from my own location, and what effect this has on my characters?
- If my script is set in another period of time, do I know enough historical details about that period in terms of language, living conditions, clothing, relationships, attitudes, and influences?
- Have I read diaries or other literature from that period so that I have a sense of how people spoke and the words they used?
- In researching my characters, have I been willing to ask for help from resource people—whether librarians or people knowledgeable about a specific area?

SUMMARY

Almost every character demands some research. There is more than one reason why new writers are often told to write about what they know. The research can be both time-consuming and expensive. Many new writers can't afford to spend a month in Africa, or may not know how to find a safecracker, or may not be able to hold out the possibility of new business to the Amish buggymaker.

Understanding the importance of research and understanding what to research are important steps in the process of creating strong characters.

Once new writers get over their initial resistance to research, many find it can be one of the most exciting, creative, and exhilarating parts of the writing process. It paves the way for the imagination to give the character life.

2

~~~

Defining the Character: Consistencies and Paradoxes

Think of someone you really like—friend, spouse, teacher, relative. The first qualities of this person that you think about may be what's consistent about his or her personality. It may be that one friend is always compassionate and empathetic, while another always enjoys a good party; perhaps a teacher is known for her logic and analysis, and a relative seems driven by a determination to win in sports and in life.

But the next thoughts you have about this person might be details that are surprising, illogical, paradoxical. Your most logical friend loves to wear those silly hats. Your most sensation-oriented friend reads books about astronomy in his spare time. And your compassionate friend hates bugs, going on the attack with flyswatter and toxic sprays whenever she hears or sees them in her home.

The defining of character is a back-and-forth process. You ask questions. You observe. You think through your own experiences, and make others up. You test these against the consistency of your character. You think of details that are unique and unpredictable.

This process may seem haphazard and, to some extent, it is. Yet there are specific qualities that are found in all dimensional characters. When your characters refuse to come to life, understanding these qualities can help you expand, enrich, and deepen them.

HOW DO YOU BEGIN?

Whether you are modeling your character on someone you know intimately, on someone you observe, on yourself, or are building a composite from a number of details, creating a character usually begins with one strong stroke. There's the first vivid image that begins to give you a sense of who your character is.

You might see the character physically—what does he look like? How does he move? Maybe you want to explore a character who's suddenly caught in a crisis. How will she act or react? You might begin with a gut feeling about what matters to this person.

There are stages to creating character. Although not necessarily in this order, these stages include:

1. Getting the first idea from observation or experience
2. Creating the first broad strokes
3. Finding the core of the character in order to create character consistency
4. Finding the paradoxes within the character to create complexity
5. Adding emotions, attitudes, and values to further round out the character
6. Adding details to make the character specific and unique

OBSERVATION

Much of the material writers use to create characters will come from observing small details.

Carl Sautter talks about observing an unusual character in a restaurant. This real-life scene helped him illustrate to a class how observation and imagination work together.

"I was doing a seminar in Washington, D.C., and we were talking about character, and the students were coming up with all the characters you'd expect—the prostitute with the heart of gold, the happy fat person who is really miserable underneath, etc. And then I went to lunch and there was a guy in this coffee shop who had a bowl of soup and a knife. I was watching him, thinking, What the hell is he dunking in there? He had a plate with a roll on it, and a pat of butter—which was obviously very cold and very hard. He ceremoniously unwrapped this butter, took his knife and stuck it in the pat of butter, and then he put it in the soup to melt it, and then he spread it on his roll. Now, logically, this makes sense—a guy is using this hot soup to melt this butter for his bread. And it got me to thinking: What is that man's personality? What does that action tell you? When I returned to the class, I mentioned this to them, and we took that scenario, and asked questions about that guy. The characters they came up with—who this guy could be, and why, and how old—were ten times better than the ideas they came up with before they had started observing."

In creating characters for advertising, observation is particularly important. Joe Sedelmaier, one of the best creators of advertising characters, observes details closely in the people he encounters. He generally casts actors based on certain idiosyncrasies he notices in their personalities, usually casting nonprofessionals because he finds them more interesting and more real. First he observes, then he converts what he has discovered from this observation into a character. When he cast Clara Peller in the Wendy's "Where's the Beef?" ad, he drew upon details he had noticed about her: "I first met Clara because we needed a manicurist for a commercial we were shooting. We went across the street, and found Clara. She didn't have a speaking role, but when I finished shooting the scene, she turned to me with that deep voice and said, 'Hi, honey, how are you?' And I thought, This is terrific. So I started using her in a number of ads. When I was asked to do the Wendy's ad, I felt that the original idea was all wrong, since it used a young couple with a big bun who said, 'Where's all the beef?' So I thought it would be funnier with two old ladies. Then the idea of Clara came to me as sort of the bull in the china shop. I could hear her say, 'Well, where's all the beef?' We started shooting, but because Clara had emphysema she had trouble with 'Where's all the . . .' By the time she got to 'beef,' it was not there, so I told her to just say 'Where's the beef?' "

INTEGRATING EXPERIENCE

Wherever you begin in the creation of your character, ultimately you will have to draw upon your own experience. There is nowhere else to turn to know whether you've got the character right. No one else can tell you whether or not you've got a character that's credible, real, and consistent. You must rely on your own inner sense of what people are all about.

Writer after writer emphasizes this aspect of writing: "Whatever I know, I know from my own experience," says James Dearden. "In the end, the writer has to draw on himself. I have Alex inside me, and Dan inside me. And if you haven't got the experience, then you have to go out and get it. All the characters I write come from me. I draw from within. I always think, How would I react in that situation?"

Carl Sautter agrees. "I think you have to find the element in characters that is you. And it isn't that every character is autobiographical but often you ask, 'Who is the character you wish you were? What do you wish you could get away with?' When you start writing stories that only you can write, you raise yourself as a writer to a whole new level. So, whatever it is, even when it's a supporting character, I try to find a part of it that I can really identify with personally."

Barry Morrow, who wrote the original screenplay of *Rain Man*, says, "Movies have to be about the things you're interested in or it's no fun to write them. In *Rain Man*, Raymond likes the things I like. He likes baseball and pancakes. And Charlie likes what I like—money and cars and women."

Ron Bass, who did the rewrites for *Rain Man*, adds, "I carry Charlie and Raymond inside of me. I have all their faults and their good points in my personality. Certainly there's a part of me that is frightened of human contact and overcompensates for that, and certainly I have all those defenses that Charlie has. And there's a part of me that's very soft and wants to be loved. Writing is a very intimate process, and I know when I've got the guy, and I know when I don't have the guy."

In television, often there's one writer on the show who represents the character. This person becomes a kind of plumb line or measure of whether the character works.

Coleman Luck, co–executive producer of "The Equalizer" and writer of a number of shows in the series, identifies with McCall. He was with the show for four years—almost from the beginning—and became a guiding force for a number of character decisions.

"Some writer on the show has to become that character," he says. "There has to be an empathy between the writer and the character. I don't think there's any other way to do this. There's something inside of me that's like McCall. I'm not McCall, I've not been a CIA agent, but I've lived a few years. I was an army officer in Vietnam and I was in combat when I was twenty-two, and I've been through a lot. I can understand his concerns, his sense of guilt, his need for forgiveness, his need for absolution. So if you don't have the experience of self-examination, and knowing yourself to some degree, you're never going to know your character. Flat out you are not."

PHYSICAL DESCRIPTION

Readers will form a visual impression of a character they meet in novels. Most novels give vivid character descriptions to give the reader an immediate sense of who this person is.

Occasionally a novel, such as *Ordinary People,* avoids physical descriptions, focusing instead on details about the character's inner life. But readers still make an imaginative leap, forming their own pictures from these psychological details.

Screenplays almost always give one or two lines of strong character details, in order to hook both the reader and potential actors.

What does a physical description do? First of all, it's evocative—it implies other aspects of the character. The reader begins to associate other qualities and imagine additional details from the few lines of description you've given.

Let your imagination play with the following description, from a script called *Fire-Eyes* by one of my clients, Roy Rosenblatt: "A sweet-faced guy who's probably done his job too long."

What other qualities come to mind? You may start thinking about his weariness. Do you wonder if he's also cynical? You probably find him likable, because of his face, but do you wonder if he has some conflict with his job or his coworkers because he's been at it too long? Maybe he suffers from burnout; perhaps you feel sorry for him, or even empathize. Can you begin to think of the way he'd walk or talk?

In novels, the character descriptions have sometimes created details that make the character instantly recognizable. Consider the descriptions of four famous detectives: Sherlock Holmes, Father Brown, Hercule Poirot, and Miss Marple.

Sherlock Holmes is described by Arthur Conan Doyle as

tall and spare with a hawklike face, wearing a deerstalker hat and a long gray traveling cloak. He is cold and precise, with extraordinary powers of observation. [1]

Father Brown, created by G. K. Chesterton, is a short, chubby Catholic priest, always carrying brown paper parcels and a large umbrella. He has a vast store of humor, wisdom, and insight into human nature. [2]

Agatha Christie's Hercule Poirot is a little Belgian detective with an egg-shaped head and a passion for order[3]; and Miss Marple is an elderly lady, "so charming, so innocent, such a fluffy and pink and white old lady, with an old-fashioned tweed coat and skirt, a couple of scarves and a small felt hat with a bird's wing."[4]

In scripts particularly, the physical description can be strengthened if it is also actable. That means that something is implied that an actor can use—some sense of the character's movement, or of a certain look, such as the hunch of the shoulders, the tilt of the head, a particular walk. Such descriptions give clues the actor can use to build the role. "Pretty" is difficult to act; "strong" and "handsome" are not very helpful.

In *Fatal Attraction*, Alex Forrest is defined in terms of a look, the kind of clothes she chooses, and a sense of attitude to her age:

> At that moment, an extremely attractive blond girl passes by. . . . She turns and gives him a look to make hell freeze over. . . . She really is sensational-looking. She must be in her thirties, but she dresses younger, trendily, and gets away with it.

Here is a description of the main character from a film called *Dance of the Damned*, written, directed, and produced by two of my clients, Katt Shea and Andy Ruben (and available on videotape). Notice how many details there are that could be helpful to the actor—details of movement, feeling, and intention. The description conveys a sense of yearning that will play throughout the film:

> The man turns away from his reflection—his acutely handsome face: ethereal, sad, with a childlike naïveté. And yet there is something in the way he moves, the tilt of his head—an alien-otherness, a catlike tentativeness, a predatory grace.

Another of my clients, Sandi Steinberg, has written one of my favorite descriptions, which gives a sense of the comic dimensions that are to come in her script, *Curses*:

> Maria-Theresa, 50's, awakens with a start, a big woman with small illusions—180 Guatemalan pounds squeezed into a pink lace teddy. She grabs a cluster of garlic to her bosom and begins to chant.

In writing actable descriptions, it's important to be both general enough that a number of actors can play the role and specific enough that there's a definite character being created. A description that evokes other qualities and associations can engage an actor's imagination, convincing him or her that this is a character worth doing.

THE CORE OF THE CHARACTER

Characters need to be consistent. This does not mean that they are predictable or stereotypical. It means that characters, like people, have a kind of core personality that defines who they are and gives us expectations about how they will act. If characters deviate from this core, they may come across as incredible, as not making sense or adding up.

As Barry Morrow explains, "Part of the appeal of characters

in a film is their predictability. You understand who they are and you have a sense of their history and their code of honor and their ethics and their world view. The character is going to have to choose and make certain choices which the audience can anticipate and enjoy watching."

Advertising executive Michael Gill concurs, and adds: "I think with characters—just like with your friends—you want a certain consistency. You don't want your friends to change every time you talk to them. You don't want them to be one place at one time and a totally different place emotionally and psychologically the next.

"What you look for is people that have known characteristics. So once you've created a successful character, then the art is to try to keep it fresh and current and at the same time maintain those consistent specific feelings and details that are very reassuring to people."

Character qualities don't exist alone. A consistent character has certain qualities that in turn imply other qualities.

For instance, let's say you're writing the next Indiana Jones story. One of your characters is a professor of religion—a man who's an expert on early Christian history who's going to hold the key to finding an important artifact. What might we expect to be true about this character?

If this religion professor has a Ph.D., we would expect that he has done a great deal of research and can easily ferret out all types of obscure information in libraries or bookstores. It would be consistent for him to be interested in related areas, such as philosophy, church history, sociology, anthropology.

Many religion professors, particularly if they've received their degrees from American universities or seminaries, have had liberal-arts backgrounds. They've taken courses in the arts, literature, probably one or two science classes. It wouldn't be inconsistent for a professor to love literature or music or art or architecture—or to be knowledgeable about these areas.

This interest in archaeology and early church history could lead to a love of travel. Perhaps he might have done some archaeological research in Turkey, or Israel, or Egypt. It wouldn't be unusual for him to know several languages, perhaps Greek, Latin, and Hebrew.

Notice how one set of characteristics implies other character qualities. A person who is sophisticated enough to know the music of Mendelssohn may also know the painting of Vermeer and Rembrandt. A person who grew up on a farm probably knows something about repairing tractors and cars, and about how to read weather patterns. A person who is a successful stockbroker probably knows something about economic patterns in Japan.

Although this all seems very obvious, many characters who are defined in one way seem to have none of the qualities one would expect from that kind of a person. There are characters who are mothers who have no awareness of a child crying across the street. There are characters who grew up in Brazil, but don't react when they hear someone speaking Portuguese at a nearby table in an Amsterdam restaurant. In television shows, I've seen characters who are supposed to have photographic memories, yet can't remember well-known dates or the composer of instantly recognizable popular music.

There's a lack of consistency in the characters in these situations. If, for some reason, the writer has deliberately set up the characters in this way, then that needs to be made clear. Otherwise it will seem as if the writer is unaware of the inconsistency.

EXERCISE: Think about what qualities you would expect to see in an art dealer, a murderer, a gas station attendant. The first qualities you think about might be the obvious ones. Brainstorm long enough to come up with qualities that would be consistent but not as obvious to the casual observer.

If you have only one or two consistent characteristics, you'll be in danger of creating a stereotype. But a consistent character need not be a limited character. By brainstorming consistencies, you can find many associations that are not stereotypical. You'll still need to select which aspects of your character you'll reveal in your story. But to the reader or audience, it will be clear that you know and understand the core makeup of this type of person.

ADDING THE PARADOX

Human nature being what it is, a character is always more than just a set of consistencies. People are illogical and unpredictable. They do things that surprise us, startle us, change all our preconceived ideas about them. Many of these characteristics we only learn about after knowing someone for a long time. These are the details that are not readily apparent, but that we find particularly compelling, that draw us toward certain people. In the same way, these paradoxes often form the basis for creating a fascinating and unique character.

Paradoxes do not negate the consistencies; they simply add to them. For instance, I once had a religion professor who specialized in the New Testament. He was a rather reserved, shy, unassuming man, with a great knowledge of his material. He had written many books, and although he was modest in class, he had a strong sense of his own scholarship. He knew what he believed, and was not averse to letting his students know where he stood on any religious issue. He could be the model for the consistent character mentioned previously.

But this professor had once been a cowboy and was an expert with the lasso. About once every three or four years, someone would talk him into showing us some of his rope tricks, which always included lassoing the leg of a willing victim. Also, besides having been a cowboy, he was known to do speed racing on the salt flats of Utah. All these characteristics made the professor a fascinating character.

Novelist Leonard Tourney says paradoxes are the crux of fascinating characters: "Characters are more interesting if they are made of mixed stuff, if they contain warring elements. To create these warring elements, you begin by establishing one, and then asking, 'Given this element, what elements are there in the same person that would create in that person a kind of conflict?' Take an element like a home-loving domestic type— this is not a conflicting element, but if on weekends he goes out with his friends and does something very physical, then that's very out of keeping with what you would expect. With that characteristic, you're moving in the direction of a character that creates interest."

Anna Phelan described some of the character paradoxes she had discovered when writing the character of Dian Fossey. Although some of these were cut from the film, Anna found them to be particularly fascinating aspects of Dian's character: "Dian was addicted to cigarettes and addicted to chocolate. She sometimes consumed fifteen to twenty Hershey bars a day. Right after she was murdered, when I was still trying to decide whether to take this assignment for this screenplay, I found out that in her closet, in this horrible, little tin cabin in the middle of the deepest part of Africa, was a green satin ball gown from Bonwit Teller. And that is what made me do the screenplay. I mean, the contradiction: what in God's name is this woman doing, living in this part of the world, with a green satin ball gown in her closet?"

In *Gone With the Wind*, we first see Scarlett as a flirt. We expect her to be seductive and manipulative—it's consistent with her character. But we might be surprised to learn that math was her favorite subject in school, that she is clearheaded in the midst of a crisis, that she is strong, determined, and shrewd.

Otto, in *A Fish Called Wanda*, is set up as dumb and jumpy

and jealous, yet he reads Nietzsche and meditates. The very competent Jane, in *Broadcast News,* spends five minutes crying every morning. All of these paradoxes round out the character.

EXERCISE: Think through your own consistencies and paradoxes. What are the consistencies and paradoxes of your friends? Of your most favorite and least favorite relatives?

ADDING VALUES, ATTITUDES, AND EMOTIONS

If you create only consistent characters, they can still be dimensional. If you add some paradoxes, your characters will become more unique. And if you want to deepen the characters further, there are other qualities that you can add. You can expand upon their emotions, their attitudes, and their values.

Emotions deepen a character's humanity. In *Working Girl,* we empathize with Tess McGill as the downtrodden secretary. When she discovers that her boss has lied to her, you can feel her discouragement, her sense of betrayal, her sadness and hopelessness. In one short emotional moment, we in the audience connect with Tess, and have a greater understanding of what moves her.

In many of the best stories, we empathize with the character. We can feel Rocky's frustration. We can feel Ben's moment of joy in *Chariots of Fire* when the race has been won. We can sense the yearning of Shane; the depression of Conrad in *Ordinary People*; the disgust Sally feels (in *When Harry Met Sally*) when she first meets Harry; and in *Dangerous Liaisons,* the self-loathing of Valmont.

The kind of emotions that are actable and understandable can be defined in a number of different ways. I've heard some psychologists humorously describe the emotions as mad, sad, glad, and scared. As a beginning list, it's not bad since each category implies other emotions.

Mad implies angry, filled with rage, peeved, frustrated, irritated, and flying off the handle.
Sad implies depressed, feeling hopeless, discouraged, self-destructive, and melancholy.
Glad implies joy, happiness, and ecstasy.
Scared implies fear, terror, horror, and anxiety.

The novel of *Ordinary People* adds emotional layering when it describes Conrad's depression:

To have a reason to get up in the morning, it is necessary to possess a guiding principle. A belief of some kind. A bumper sticker, if you will. . . . Lying on his back in bed, he gazes around the walls of his room, musing about what has happened to his collection of statements. Gone now. . . . Instead, the walls are bare. They have been freshly painted. Pale blue. An anxious color. Anxiety is blue; failure, gray. He knows those shades. He told Crawford they would be back to sit on the end of his bed, paralyzing him, shaming him. . . .[5]

In my consulting, when I find emotional layering missing from a character, I often recommend that the writer go through the story and ask what each character is feeling in each scene. Although not all the answers need to be layered into the script, understanding the emotions can produce a much richer character and a much deeper scene.

Attitudes convey opinions, the point of view, the particular slant that a character takes in a certain situation. They deepen and define a character, showing how a character looks at life.
Novels, in particular, can convey attitudes because of the

subjective nature of their approach. The writer is able to get behind the character's eyes, to see the world through his or her point of view.

In the novel of *Witness,* we can see Rachel's attitude toward the funeral of her husband, Jacob.

> Rachel Lapp, seated on a straight chair facing the coffin, her back to the preacher, listened closely and tried to take solace from the preacher's words. An Amish funeral was supposed to be a celebration of sorts. Another Christian victory. But Rachel had sometimes found the spirit of the thing a bit difficult to summon up. Even when the decedent had lived a long and happy life, as was so often the case among the Amish, dead was still dismal as far as Rachel was concerned, and no amount of preachment could redress it.[6]

The world of the funeral is seen from Rachel's point of view, giving the reader insight into Rachel's attitude toward death. This short paragraph also implies a spirit of rebellion, since Rachel does not see death with the same spirit that other Amish do. This attitude will lead her to make some un-Amish decisions, such as visiting her sister in Baltimore, wanting to delay remarriage, and even dancing in the barn with John Book.

Characters have attitudes toward each other, toward themselves, toward the situation, toward particular issues. In the "Mama Said" episode of "Murphy Brown," written by Diane English, Murphy's mother comes to town, and everyone has an attitude.

When Murphy introduces her mother to the staff, they convey their attitude toward Murphy through their surprise.

FRANK
Your mother? Wow, Murph. You've got a mother.

Murphy's mother, Avery, conveys her attitude toward her ex-husband.

JIM
So tell me, Mrs. Brown. Is Mr. Brown here as well?

AVERY
No. Mr. Brown is in Chicago with a woman half his age. We've been divorced for 15 years. I got the house and a lot of money. He got his underwear and the asphalt on the driveway.

Murphy conveys her attitude toward her mother's visit.

MURPHY
If we both made up a list of our favorite things to do, "visit each other" would be about tied with "eat head cheese."

Corky conveys her attitude about what kind of relationships mothers and daughters are supposed to have.

CORKY
So tell me, what kinds of plans do you two have for your first night together?

AVERY
. . . I thought Murphy would like to join me for dinner . . . then I'll just go back to my hotel.

CORKY
Hotel? . . . Murphy! You're making your mother stay in a hotel?

Phil the bartender has an attitude toward Avery.

                    PHIL
Damn good-looking woman. . . . She's got good
calves.

And Avery has an attitude toward her daughter and herself.

                    AVERY
You are my greatest achievement. But somewhere
along the line, I lost you and I never got you back.
I know you must be surprised to hear your mother
admitting a failure.

Diane English says that attitudes are a key to the comedy—
and the drama—of a situation. "We often ask, 'What attitude is
that character bringing into the situation?' If the attitudes
aren't clear, the script can be flat and bland. The funniness
comes from heightened attitudes that emanate from a situation
as it becomes complicated by events.

"We wrote a scene that involved Miles and Murphy. He has
to try to convince her to use the FYI lawyers and not handle the
matter herself. When we first wrote it, it was quite dull. Miles
had no attitude. He was simply a messenger of information and
there was nothing funny about that. We couldn't find an attitude in that situation, so we had him walk into the scene having
had a new haircut. He comes in trying to convince her to see a
lawyer and all the time she's just staring at his hair. He's very
self-conscious that he has to convince her to do this and he
knows his hair looks horrible and he's trying to pretend that it
doesn't. He had an attitude so we got comedy, and we got
something out of the character instead of him just coming in
and laying this information out on the table."

EXERCISE: Think about the attitudes and perspectives from
the last film you saw or the last book you read. Did you clearly
understand the character's point of view about ideas, philosophies, or situations in the film? Think about other films. Do you

understand how Karen Blixen feels about the Africans in *Out of Africa*? Do you understand James Bond's sense of justice? Are you clear about Harry's and Sally's perspectives on love and friendship? Do you know what Rhett Butler thinks about the Civil War?

Even though the story might not tell you a character's attitudes in a straightforward way, it should imply it—so you can sense the character's perspective.

Values expressed by a character may be an opportunity for writers to express what they believe. Sometimes these values—and concerns, philosophies, and belief systems—are ones they've observed, which fit the character, but do not necessarily convey their own perspective.

In this scene from *Witness,* notice how Rachel carries a personal value (in this case, about guns in the house) as well as the Amish value toward violence:

Rachel comes in after John Book has been showing his gun to Samuel.

> RACHEL
> John Book, while you are in this house, I insist
> that you respect our ways.

> JOHN
> Right. Here. Put it somewhere where it's safe.
> Where he won't find it.

This scene is followed by one between Samuel and Eli. In this scene, Eli carries the values of the community:

> ELI
> The gun—that gun of the hand is for the taking of
> human life. Would you kill another man?

Samuel stares at it, not meeting his grandfather's eyes. Eli leans forward, extends his hands ceremonially.

ELI
What you take into your hands, you take into your heart.

A beat, then Samuel musters some defiance.

SAMUEL
I would only kill a bad man.

ELI
Only a bad man. I see. And you know these bad men on sight? You are able to look into their hearts and see this badness?

SAMUEL
I can see what they do. I have *seen* it.

ELI
And having seen, you would become one of them? So that the one goes into the other into the other, into the other . . . ?

He breaks off, bows his head for a moment. Then he fixes the boy with a stern eye and, driving the heel of his palm firmly into the tabletop, with enormous intensity:

ELI
(continuing)
"Wherefore come out from among them and be ye separate, saith the Lord!"
(indicating pistol, continuing from
Corinthians 6:17)
"And touch not the unclean thing!"

Many films deal with a recognition that some values are worth fighting for and dying for. *Silkwood, The China Syndrome*, and the Indiana Jones films all revolve around characters who are driven by what they value.

Many films deal with characters at a time of crisis when they must make moral choices, confronting their values and choosing those they will live by.

The Breakfast Club shows four people dealing with their identities. *The Journey of Natty Gann* deals with a crisis that leads to a girl's search for her father. In both *Absence of Malice* and *The Accused* we see a character who learns integrity during the course of the film.

In *Dead Poets Society,* we learn about the value of *carpe diem*—"seize the day"—and about sucking the marrow of life.

Besides these life themes, there are other driving forces that control characters. The search for forgiveness, the desire for reconciliation, the yearning for love or home can be found in many films ranging from *Shane* to *A Fish Called Wanda* to *E.T.*

Incorporating values into particular characters does not mean that your characters need to *discuss* what they believe. Instead, you communicate values through what the character does, through conflict, and through character attitudes.

DETAILING THE CHARACTER

If you infuse your characters with an emotional life, with specific attitudes and values, they will be multidimensional. But there is another step that can make the character original and unique. That is adding the details.

Behavior—the way people do things—marks the difference between two people who might be similar in physical appearance or outlook. People have distinguishing characteristics, small details that make them singular and special.

If I were to make a list of some details I've noticed about my friends and acquaintances, it would include:

[41]

- A person who says "you know" and "for sure" in every sentence
- A thirty-year-old woman who carries two stuffed animals in her handbag, and makes origami cranes as gifts for people she meets
- A thirty-five-year-old man who never wears suits because of his anti-establishment bias
- A forty-year-old man who always has jazz music playing in the background
- A professional woman who is known for her unusual earrings (worn only among friends) of bananas, flamingos, cockatoos, and boomerangs

Some of the most memorable characters are remembered because of such details: Murphy Brown breaks number-2 pencils when she's under stress; Indiana Jones hates snakes, and always wears his favorite hat; Archie Bunker's pet name for his son-in-law is "Meathead."

Details can be actions, behaviors, use of language, gestures, the clothes one wears, the way a person laughs, the unusual approaches the person takes to a situation.

These details often come from the person's imperfections. In *The Power of Myth*, Joseph Campbell says, "The writer must be true to truth. And that's a killer, because the only way you can describe a human being truly is by describing his imperfections. The perfect human being is uninteresting. . . . It is the imperfections of life that are lovable. . . . Perfection is a bore, it's inhuman. The umbilical point, the humanity, the thing that makes you human and not supernatural and immortal . . . the imperfection, striving, living . . . that's what's lovable."[7]

We can see these human imperfections in such critically acclaimed films as *A Fish Called Wanda* (Ken stutters), *sex, lies and videotape* (the lead character is consumed by thoughts of garbage), and *When Harry Met Sally.* In this last film, written by Nora Ephron, Harry talks about the unique details that make up Sally's personality.

INT. NEW YEAR'S EVE PARTY—NIGHT

HARRY

I've been doing a lot of thinking. And the thing is,
I love you . . . I love how you get cold when it's 71
degrees out. I love that it takes you an hour to
order a sandwich. I love that you get a little crin-
kle right there when you're looking at me like I'm
nuts. I love that after I spend the day with you I
can still smell your perfume on my clothes. And I
love that you're the last person I want to talk to
before I go to sleep at night. And it's not because
it's New Year's Eve. I came here tonight because
when you realize you want to spend the rest of
your life with somebody, you want the rest of your
life to start as soon as possible.

EXERCISE: Think about your friends and acquaintances.
What small details distinguish them and make them memorable? Which of these details are endearing? Which are annoy-
ing? How might you incorporate them into a character?

A CASE STUDY: "MIDNIGHT CALLER"

"Midnight Caller" premiered in the fall of 1988. The creator of
the series, Richard DiLello, discusses the creation of the complex character of Jack Killian:

"I always start with a character's name. I'll spend a couple of
days writing lists of names. I figured Jack Killian was a man in
his thirties. In his backstory, I wanted to have some major
event occur in his life that would bring him from being a cop to
this other place where he wound up—as the Nighthawk. I
thought that killing his own partner would be the most extreme. I was afraid that this might be too big a leap for the
audience to take, but then I realized that you needed that one
moment in the dark when you couldn't turn back the clock.

[43]

"In the pilot, there are two terse scenes which show him losing himself in a conventional way, going into the bottom of the bottle and cutting himself off from the rest of the world. The character of Devon King comes in and redeems him. She's the one who gives him a chance to come down from the crucifix where he has nailed himself.

"In some ways, Jack is a typical cop. He's blue-collar. He doesn't have a formal education. Face it, you don't get out of Harvard Business School and become a police officer. He likes sports and rock and roll.

"His own eclectic reading makes him different and sensitive to the world. He reads contemporary fiction—I had always imagined he'd be a great fan of Jack Kerouac and Raymond Carver. Killian is trying to form his own philosophy in life. He is not a conscious intellectual; he's more of a street intellectual. He operates from his gut. He shoots from the hip and makes a lot of mistakes. But he's totally different because most cops become totally cynical. They walk in the blackness of their own work and basically leave humanity. But he's always remained sympathetic and caring of other people's problems. Maybe he can't deal with a lot of his own problems so he finds it easier to help others. He can't organize his own life very well. He can't find a stable relationship with someone else but he can certainly help you find one and tell you what to do.

"I think he realizes that there was more in life he could have gone for and opportunities to socialize were missed. He's more emotionally expressive than most cops—not stoic or repressed—and he doesn't like it about himself; he'd prefer to be a little cooler. But he's responsive, he gets angry at the pomposity in other people, at their hypocrisy, at injustice and the things that aren't fair. He gets frustrated with having to deal with the bureaucracy. What he likes are the simple things—a good meal, listening to Elvis Presley records, seeing the Chicago Cubs do well.

"He's definitely a loner, but he'd prefer not being a loner. The great love of his life has AIDS, and he's angry at the man who knowingly gave it to her. His emotional life is still growing.

"Killian works out of his own moral imperative, his own set of values. His humanity is the most important thing about this show. His attitude is always humanistic, but sometimes masked by a touch of black humor. Jack definitely is filling the function of helping the audience understand their world. At the end of every show when Jack signs off he makes a statement about what he's learned in that hour. It was always my intention that he was, in fact, heroic—but a different kind of hero. His summing up at the end shows him to be a man of thought as well as of action."

APPLICATION

Since much of character creation comes from observation, a writer is continually "in training." As an exercise, study a character at the airport, at the grocery store, or in your work environment. Ask yourself the following questions:

- If I were to describe this character in a strong, broad stroke, what would that description be?
- What might I expect to be true of this person, given his or her context? Can you imagine paradoxes that might make an interesting character?

Then, as you look at the main characters in your story, ask yourself:

- Do my characters "make sense"? Have I shown a number of qualities that my characters might have?
- What makes my characters interesting? Compelling? Fascinating? Different? Unpredictable? Do my characters do the unexpected at times? Do these paradoxes contradict any of the consistent qualities I've created, or are they used to expand my characters?

- What are my characters concerned about? Are these values understandable? Are they conveyed through action and attitudes, rather than through long monologues?
- Is it clear how my characters feel? Does each individual character have a broad range of emotions, rather than repeating the same ones?
- Have I used my characters' attitudes to help define character?

The process of creating character is ongoing. Even when not writing, writers need to store up details, looking to reality for inspiration and ideas. As advertising director Joe Sedelmaier says, "It always starts in reality. If I'm gonna copy, I'm gonna copy reality."

SUMMARY

Barry Morrow says creating a character is similar to the work of an artist: "It's like shaping a lump of clay, or like whittling a stick. You can't get to the fine stuff until you get the bark off of it."

Shaping the clay of your character is a six-step process:

1. Through observation and experience, you begin to form an idea of a character.
2. The first broad strokes begin to define the character.
3. You define the character's consistency, so the character makes sense.
4. Adding quirks, the illogical, the paradoxical, makes the character fascinating and compelling.
5. The qualities of emotions, values, and attitudes deepen the character.
6. Adding details makes the character unique and special.

Creating the Backstory

When you first meet someone in real life, are you often curious about the person's background? Have you ever asked these kinds of questions:

- Where was he from? Why did he move to your city?
- Why did she decide to take this particular job? What jobs has she had in the past?
- How long have they been married? Where did they meet?

We're curious about the past, because we know there are interesting stories behind every decision. Some might involve intrigue ("She was forced to leave town"), or romance ("They met at the top of the Eiffel Tower when they were both students in France"), or corruption ("The politician used government money to pay for his Bel Air home"). The current situation is a result of decisions and events from the past. And the choices that have been made will determine other choices in the future.

Every novel and screenplay focuses on a specific story, one

we might call the *front story*. That's the real story the writer wants to tell. But the characters in the front story do what they do and are what they are because of their past. This past might include traumas and crises, important people who came into their lives, the negative and positive feedback they've received, childhood dreams and goals, and of course influences from society and culture.

The *backstory* provides two different types of information. One is the past events and influences that directly affect the construction of the story. Films and books such as *Sibyl*, *The Three Faces of Eve*, *Hamlet*, *Ordinary People*, and *Citizen Kane* all have crucial backstory events that created the front story. Both audience/reader and writer must be aware of these events to understand the story.

Some backstory information is part of the character biography. This information may never be conveyed to the audience, but the writer needs to know it to help create the character.

Characters are born in a writer's mind and are given a specific set of attitudes and experiences. The backstory helps the writer discover which of these attitudes and experiences are essential in order to fully create the character.

WHAT BACKSTORY INFORMATION DO YOU NEED TO KNOW?

Many actors do considerable work upon the backstory of their characters before playing a role. The famous actor, director, and teacher Constantin Stanislavski recommended that actors write out specific biographies about their characters. Lajos Egri, in his book *The Art of Dramatic Writing*, recommends that writers do the same. A character biography might include the following information:

PHYSIOLOGY: Age, Sex, Posture, Appearance, Physical Defects, Heredity.

SOCIOLOGY: Class, Occupation, Education, Home Life, Religion, Political Affiliations, Hobbies, Amusements.

PSYCHOLOGY: Sex Life and Moral Standards, Ambitions, Frustrations, Temperament, Attitude toward Life, Complexes, Abilities, I.Q., Personality (extravert, introvert). [1]

Carl Sautter comments on this approach: "There is a danger to doing the three-page character biography. I still encourage writers to do it, but then I basically tell them to throw it away. Do it and know all of that but let other elements evolve as your character evolves. In a lot of ways that character is being born in front of you. Anybody can come up with a three-page history for a character, and you do find lots of good and useful elements through that exercise that you're able to use later on. But it can't stop there."

Frank Pierson (*Dog Day Afternoon, Cool Hand Luke, In Country*) adds: "What you need to know about the characters is what the actors need to know to play the scenes. What is important are the sense memories. It is not important what happened to them but how they felt about it. If you want to ask questions, don't ask the characters questions like: 'What school did they go to? Did you ever work in a factory? Was your mother a domineering woman?' . . . What you want to ask the characters is, 'What was your most embarrassing moment? Did you ever feel like a fool? What are the worst things that ever happened to you? Did you ever throw up in a public place?' You need to bring out those emotions, because those are what a character carries into a scene and colors everything he does."[2]

The backstory will be different for every character. The biography by itself won't always give you relevant information. If you're writing *Hamlet*, it's not necessary to know what childhood games Hamlet played, or who was his childhood sweetheart. If you're writing *Fiddler on the Roof,* this information may be essential.

[49]

For many writers, the process of creating backstory begins first with creating a character and beginning to work on the story. As they write, they realize they don't have certain information they need about their character. Or they discover that their character is having unexpected reactions to events and people. Perhaps they don't know how their character would respond in particular circumstances. The backstory is discovered by a process of asking Why and What questions about their character.

- Why did Karen Blixen go to Africa? What was it in her life in Denmark that motivated her to move?
- Why was Alex in *Fatal Attraction* so desperate to marry Dan and have a child? What influences in her life led her—at the age of thirty-six—to the point of madness?
- Why is Beth in *Ordinary People* so afraid of feelings? What was she like when her children were young, when she couldn't control everything?
- What in Murphy Brown's past led her to become an alcoholic?
- Why did Bruce Wayne become Batman?

Getting to know the backstory of a character is similar to getting to know the past of a new friend. The information from the past deepens the relationship. Coleman Luck describes backstory in this way: "You start by looking at your character as having a fully faceted life—a life that needs to be explored. It's like going back and discovering your grandfather. Are you going to sit there and define him by listening to all the facts about him . . . or by asking key questions to try to find the essence of his character?"

Finding the backstory is a process of discovery. You begin by asking questions of your character. Then you go back to try to figure out what happened in the past that might influence decisions and actions in the present.

When Bill Kelley and Earl Wallace were writing *Witness*, Bill wondered why John Book didn't have a woman in his life. He asked Earl, and together they tried to construct an answer.

"John Book was something of an enigma," Bill says. "He didn't seem to have a great deal of romantic experience; so I asked Earl, 'Why doesn't he?' and Earl said, 'Well, he doesn't have time—he's busy.' And I said, 'Come on, Earl, I know two of the busiest cops in L.A. and they have plenty of time for romance and they're both married.' So he says, 'Well, he's not a prude,' which helped define him for me. Earl did most of the work on John Book in the script, but when I started writing the novel, I had to define him even more closely. Gradually, I turned him into sort of a stiff-back, not really available to romance, the sort of person who kept asking incisive questions and scaring women off. You know Rachel may have been only the third woman in his life—ever, and that includes his sister."

James Dearden explains Alex Forrest's character: "Alex had had a long affair with an older married man which ended about six months before the story began. She thought he was going to marry her, but he didn't, so she was on the rebound. Originally there was a scene in the film about her loneliness, and about this affair, but we took it out."

Backstory information does not always have to appear in the story. In both these examples, the writer needed to know backstory information to understand the character; but it was not necessary to the story line.

Kurt Luedtke explains: "I don't think we ever do enough work on backstory. I've never known a situation where backstory was completely solved before writing the screenplay. You think you have it down but as you go down the road you see a situation and realize you don't know where that attitude comes from. Sometimes a scene will feel flat, partly because it's clear what the character is going to do. Sometimes I'll ask, 'What if he doesn't do this particular thing that most people would do? What if she doesn't say what you expect—but the opposite?'

And sometimes, one in four times, it gets interesting. And that requires more exploration of backstory."

WHAT DOES BACKSTORY REVEAL?

Backstory helps us understand why characters behave as they do. Sometimes it gives us information about the past that helps us to understand the psychology of the character in the present.

In *Fatal Attraction*, while running with Alex in the park, Dan falls down and plays "dead." His action brings out information about her backstory:

> ALEX
>
> That was a shitty thing to do.

> DAN
>
> Hey, I'm sorry. I was just fooling around.

> ALEX
>
> My father died of a heart attack. I was seven years old. It happened right in front of me.

Knowing this piece of information helps us understand much of Alex's behavior. As a result of the death of the most important male figure in her life at an early age, she distrusts men yet feels dependent upon them. The trauma—particularly if he did die in front of her—contributes to her sense of fear and insecurity. Although Alex denies her father's death minutes later, Dan discovers that it was true. This important childhood event answers the question of why Alex reacts the way she does.

In the play *Les Liaisons Dangereuses* (*Dangerous Liaisons*), the Marquise explains how her social context determined her attitudes:

VALMONT: I often wonder how you managed to invent yourself.

MERTEUIL: I had no choice, did I, I'm a woman. Women
are obliged to be far more skilful than men. . . . You can ruin us
whenever the fancy takes you: all we can achieve by denounc-
ing you is to enhance your prestige. . . . So of course I had to
invent: not only myself, but ways of escape no one else has ever
thought of, not even I, because I had to be fast enough on my
feet to know how to improvise. And I've succeeded, because I
always knew I was born to dominate your sex and avenge my
own. . . . When I came out into society I'd already realised that
the role I was condemned to, namely to keep quiet and do as I
was told, gave me the perfect opportunity to listen and pay
attention: not to what people told me, which was naturally of
no interest, but to whatever it was they were trying to hide. I
practised detachment. . . . I consulted the strictest moralists to
learn how to appear; philosophers to find out what to think; and
novelists to see what I could get away with. And finally I was
well placed to perfect my techniques.[3]

In the novel *Ordinary People*, by Judith Guest, we gain
insight into Beth's need to control, through the backstory. This
helps explain her inability to deal with the tragedy of her son's
death.

The information comes through Calvin's point of view:

He [Calvin] can remember a period of their lives when
she [Beth] felt distinctly trapped. When Jordan was two
years old, with Connie toddling around after him at ten
months, both of them spreading havoc in that tiny north-
side apartment. "Those first five years just passed in a
blur!" he has heard her say gaily at parties. But he
remembers them, and remembers the scene: her figure,
tense with fury as she scrubbed the fingermarks from
the walls; she bursting suddenly into tears because of a

toy left out of place, or a spoonful of food thrown onto the floor from the high chair. And it did not pay him to become exasperated with her. Once he had done so, had shouted at her to forget the damned cleaning schedule for once. She had flown into a rage, railed at him, and flung herself across the bed, in hysterics. Everything had to be perfect, never mind the impossible hardship it worked on her, on them all; never mind the utter lack of meaning in such perfection.[4]

Backstory information can tell us why a character is afraid to love (perhaps because of a past hurt), or why he or she may have become cynical (perhaps because of the death of a loved one). It can give us insights into motives and actions and responses. It shows us that it's the specific influences in the past that create a very specific character in the present.

HOW MUCH BACKSTORY INFORMATION DO YOU NEED?

Many writers make the mistake of including too much backstory information. Through the use of flashbacks, voice-overs, dream sequences, they overload the script with information about the past, rather than focusing on the present.

What is dramatic is the present—the now. What is past is never as dramatic, even though it can impact on present behavior.

Carl Sautter says, "What we need to see is how this character reacts now, and if you as the writer know why he's doing it—because of some event in the past—fine. But you don't need to explain it to the audience."

Telling the audience everything about the character's past can get in the way of what is really important—the revelation of the character in the present. Backstory does not need to be talked about a great deal. Characters who have to sit down and tell about their past life tend to be boring, bland, undynamic. Long monologues, flashbacks, and exposition that give too much backstory information can be deadly, pushing the story backward rather than driving it forward into the future.

Remember the metaphor of the iceberg? Ninety percent of the backstory need not be in the script, but it should be known by the writer. The audience needs to only know enough to understand what's driving the character and will intuit a sense of the past through the character's present behavior. The richer the backstory, the richer the character.

Usually, backstory works best when it comes out a little at a time, in short pieces of dialogue. As in the examples above, the incorporation of backstory needs to be subtle, concise, and carefully worked out to illuminate and enhance the front story.

BACKSTORY IN THE NOVEL

Backstory works in similar ways in the novel, although it may be incorporated in a different form. As research for this book, I took four Santa Barbara novelists to lunch, and discussed with them ways to work with backstory in the novel. Since they are also writing teachers, they were able to give specific suggestions for both new and experienced writers.

Leonard Tourney: "The nineteenth-century novelist almost always put the backstory first—they began with the character's childhood. They had all the time in the world to explore the character, that's why the novels were so long. There's hardly a modern novel that works that way. The modern novel is front-loaded and works more like a film: the story has started before the credits come on. Most modern novels are cinematic."

Dennis Lynds, author of *Castrata* and *Why Girls Ride Side-saddle*, who writes under the pen name of Michael Collins: "What counts is the story you're telling. The backstory has to accommodate itself to your story. As I'm going along, I'll think I know what the past is, but something may happen in the present, and I'll say, 'No, I have to change the past.'

"Sometimes when we speak of backstory, we act as if it exists. But it's made up—it comes out of our imagination. As writers, we just put things on paper, and manipulate them. It's like taking clay—and layering and texturing the character. We make it up. It's not dramatic until you need it. It becomes important at a certain point, but not before."

Shelley Lowenkopf, writer of such mystery and suspense novels as *City of Hope* and *Love of the Lion*: "After you figure out who all of the characters are and what they want, and have decided what their relationships are with one another—then you can begin working with backstory. Backstory has to be woven through the back door. When I work with backstory, I fill in the background of all the characters as I go along. Backstory information is not important—until you need it! It's crucial to understand that something happened earlier, that some past event has explained motivation in the present. But you do not proceed chronologically."

Gayle Stone: "When you first start writing, you can get very confused because there's so much to be aware of. Often you feel out of control, and miserable. So as a new writer, you need to know as much as possible about the backstory, because that knowledge acts like a security blanket. Later, as you become a more experienced writer, you won't need to know so much. As a developed writer, you must know certain things to get started, but you discover who the character is by throwing him or her into situations. I don't want to know everything about my character before I begin, because I want that spark, that surprising element that happens in the process."

BACKSTORY IN SERIES TELEVISION

Some television series—"Dear John," "Gilligan's Island," "The Fugitive," "The Beverly Hillbillies," among them—begin with a short under-credit backstory sequence, since the audience must know the backstory to understand the situation. Other series look to the backstory for story ideas and character development. In some episodes, a person from the past will become the focus of the story. As in feature films, sometimes a character reacts in a particular way, as a result of some experience from the past. The more backstory information there is, the more potential there is to create a complex character with the ability to interest audiences week after week.

Coleman Luck talks about why Robert McCall, the Equalizer, was a particularly complex character: "When creating a character for a series, you need to create one who has that potential inside of them—to continually find something fresh. Robert McCall has been in the CIA. He's been a top agent around the world. He's left it. He's totally disgusted by it now—he's enraged. Those facts create a whole set of whys and its those whys that you have to figure out. That's the road map that unlocks the series to you."

These "whys" were further explored in the series by having an ongoing character from McCall's past. Control, who was McCall's nemesis, provided opportunities to explore this character complexity:

"McCall and Control have a multifaceted relationship. When you have a deep and multifaceted character like McCall, it's wonderful to bring in another character that brings a world of experience from their past. They've known each other over many years, so you can tap into anger and caring and all those many feelings that make conflict and relationships."

In "Moonlighting," the writers tapped into undiscovered areas of David's background to further expand his character. Carl Sautter explains: "One season we discovered that David had been married. It was a discovery that made sense and was usable to construct a particular episode. Most of the backstory unfolded as we worked on it.

"This information came out as an interesting story idea. We were surprised to realize that there was an ex-wife. In our discussions we learned that it was a very painful separation, so David was handling it as if she didn't exist. And so it became a terrific story about David by the fact that there is suddenly an ex-wife—with a good reason why we hadn't heard of her before."

WHICH SITUATIONS
NEED BACKSTORY INFORMATION?

Although you don't need to know everything about a character's past, there are certain situations where it's necessary to incorporate some backstory information.

If a character is going through major changes in the present, there often needs to be some backstory information to help clarify these actions and decisions.

In many Charles Bronson films, backstory explains why he's seeking revenge—usually because of some vicious crime in the past that has not been solved and avenged by the proper authorities. In many of the Sylvester Stallone or Chuck Norris films, backstory explains why these men are risking their lives for a particular mission. In films such as *The Karate Kid* or *Murphy's Romance,* we learn through backstory information why the characters decided to move from one place to another. In the pilot episode of "The Equalizer," backstory explained why Robert McCall decided to change jobs.

Life transitions don't come out of nowhere, but are motivated by certain situations in the past. If a character does something unusual or incredible, or seemingly out of character, backstory will be needed to help explain this behavior.

If an ordinary housewife in your story suddenly, without explanation, decides to spend the next few months of her life solving a crime, there had better be information in the backstory that explains not only why she's doing it, but why she might expect to solve a crime that the police can't solve.

You could, of course, show the crime in the front story, and show her husband or lover or child as the victim, thereby establishing a personal reason for her involvement. But you might also decide that in her backstory she was a law student, good at research and knowledgeable about the workings of the law; or that she is a longtime detective-story buff, or she is a member of Amnesty International and has a strong sense of justice; or perhaps her father was a cop; or her mother the victim of a crime that was never solved.

All of this backstory information can help explain behavior that is not normally in keeping with a character. A detective working on a crime case needs little backstory information to explain it. A housewife would need considerably more motivational information to explain why she is taking this action.

EXERCISE: Consider creating a character who, at the beginning of the story, decides to journey to India to seek a rare Hindu art object. What information would you want to know about the backstory and character biography? What information would the audience need to know? What would you need to know about motivation? Vocation or avocational interests? Special skills or talents? Any special situation such as a crisis point or a competition or an assignment? Why must the character take this journey now? How might the backstory information change if it took place in 1920 or 1820?

A CASE STUDY: "MURPHY BROWN"

"Murphy Brown" debuted on November 14, 1988. The first words we heard about Murphy Brown in the pilot episode were all backstory. We learned that Murphy is returning from a "drying out" period at the Betty Ford Center. In a recent interview, Diane English explained this attention to the backstory:

"Murphy's stay at the Betty Ford Center and her character as an addictive personality explained a great deal about her. It meant she would be compulsive, even cranky sometimes. By meeting her the day she returned from the Betty Ford Center, we would see her as an interviewer being tested, without any crutch to rely upon. That's what the pilot was all about—the testing of the character and the character trying to redefine herself."

So the first information about Murphy concerned the immediate backstory. It set up the situation. But the backstory was also used to expand her character.

"In this first episode, we found out she was very, very successful. Before she even entered the room I wanted to give a little backstory without having it come from her, so we heard some of the characters talking about her. She once stood up Warren Beatty. She's an ex-smoker and ex-drinker. I wanted to paint a picture of someone extremely famous, but who took no guff from anyone, a person who was probably a pain in the neck to a lot of people, but they were fond of her. That told you that she was a character we should like and we should root for her.

"In the pilot we found out she was an only child. She doesn't know how to share. She fended for herself. We felt we had to do something with a parent since we were all eager to know more about where this person came from. When we introduced her mother, it told us so much about Murphy and where she got her personality from. Her mother was an even bigger-than-life character than Murphy. Murphy felt small when she was with her mother, and inadequate. Most important, she had never said 'I love you' to her mother as an adult. That was the heart of the story.

"In one episode we brought back her ex-husband, to whom she was married for five days. This helped reveal more about Murphy's life in the sixties when she met this guy and they were both radicals and very impulsive and got married and five days later it was over. There's never been this kind of person in her life since, and just the idea that she might see him after twenty years put her in an absolute tizzy. It raised all sorts of questions for her: Am I still attractive? Is he still attractive? What will he think of my life now? Have I sold out?"

A flashback sequence in one episode was used to show Murphy getting her job: "This episode took the character back to 1977 when she and Frank were auditioning for FYI. In this episode you could see her edges—she was smoking and drinking and had frizzy hair. She was dressed in an Annie Hall hat and sneakers, and was denying that she really wanted the job and refusing to do things in the accepted way."

But backstory is useful for more than just the major character. In "Murphy Brown," backstory is also used to expand other characters: "I think we'd like to know more about Jim Dial—what his marriage is like, does he have kids, what his personal life is like outside the office, and what he's like when he lets his hair down. Corky, the same thing. She comes from Southern roots—we'd like to know more about that. We'd like to know more about Miles's backstory. How did he get that job at the age of twenty-five? What kind of family does he come from? Are they proud of him, or not? Does he have brothers and sisters? We're thinking about bringing a brother on for an episode—who is a year older than Miles and starts dating Murphy.

"We also want to meet Murphy's father. He's divorced from the mother, and he married a much younger woman. Now they have an eight-month-old baby. We expect to have a show where they visit each other. Since Murphy was an only child this introduced an interesting dynamic. She now has a stepbrother, and her father's wife is probably her age or younger than she.

"I think you define characters by putting them into situations that force them to open up a new dynamic. You can't put a character onstage and let her state what she's all about. That's externalizing. The more successful way of developing characters is actually to create a situation in which they have to react and the way they react is the way you get to know them."

In the case of "Murphy Brown," backstory has helped the

show define and expand the main character, and has created strong character relationships.

APPLICATION

As you develop the backstory of your characters, ask yourself the following questions:

- Is my work with backstory a process of discovery? Am I careful to let the backstory unfold, rather than imposing facts and history on my character that may not be relevant to my story?
- When I work backstory information into the story, am I being especially careful to tell only absolutely necessary and relevant information? Am I layering this information throughout the story, rather than confining it to one or two long speeches?
- Am I working on telling backstory information in the shortest, most concise manner possible? Am I trying to phrase the information so that one sentence can reveal a great deal, in terms of motivation, attitudes, emotions, and decisions?

SUMMARY

Finding the backstory is a process of discovery. The writer needs to work back and forth constantly—asking questions about the past to further understand the present. This process continues throughout the writing of the story. Backstory continually enriches, expands, and deepens the character. It is often the key to creating a credible character.

4

~~~

Understanding Character Psychology

You don't need to be a psychologist to understand what drives and motivates your character. Judith Guest is a novelist known for her psychological insight. Yet she's had very little background in psychology: "My formal training in psychology is minimal. I took one course in college—the psychology of the deviant individual. As a result of that class, I found I was consumed by a fascination with human behavior. I want to turn it over and upside down, and find out why people do the things they do, and why they're motivated to behave the way they do."

Just as part of constructing a character involves creating the outer character of physicality and behavior, it also involves understanding the inner workings of the character—the psychology.

A writer needs to understand what makes people tick, to know why people do what they do, want what they want. "Half of writing is psychology," says Barry Morrow. "There's a consistent core, or a consistent unity to behavior. People don't act willy-nilly. To be consistent with human behavior you have to know what people will do in most situations. People don't act without a reason. Every action has motivation and intention."

Often when we think about character psychology, we think about the abnormal personalities in films such as *Sybil, The Three Faces of Eve, David and Lisa, I Never Promised You a Rose Garden,* or *Rain Man.* But underlying motives and unconscious forces are important with any character you create.

To understand how character psychology might be constructed, let's look more closely at the two *Rain Man* characters Charlie Babbitt and Raymond Babbitt. Although Raymond is the character who demanded the most specialized research, understanding Charlie's psychology was at least as important—since it drove the story. Throughout this chapter, we will hear from the writers on the project: Barry Morrow, who created the story, and Ron Bass, who did the rewrites.

"When Steven Spielberg came on the project [Spielberg was one of the several directors slated to do the picture before Barry Levinson], we discussed Charlie as analogous to an autistic personality," says Ron Bass. "We looked on the film as a story about two autistic brothers, one who was clinically autistic and the other who had all the levels of autistic features that so-called normal people have. The universal story of *Rain Man* is about how difficult it is to make human connection, yet how necessary it is. We tell ourselves that we can live without it and that we're better off without it and that we're safe and more secure behind our defenses—but we're wrong."

We can better understand the psychology of Charlie and Raymond by looking at four key psychological areas that define the inner character. They are: the inner backstory, the unconscious, the character types, and the abnormal psychology. These are the most important for the creation of any character.

Much of the material presented in this chapter you may already be familiar with, either intuitively or from studying psychology. Understanding these categories is important, but it's just as important to remember that characters are always more than their psychology. They are constructed not clinically but imaginatively. A familiarity with these areas can shed light on the character. It can help you solve character problems, add dimension, and answer the questions, Would my character do that? Say that? React that way?

HOW THE INNER BACKSTORY DEFINES CHARACTER

In Chapter Three, we looked at some external circumstances that influence the character, including past events. The ways people internalize these events, sometimes repressing them or redefining them, based on the negative or positive emotional effect they've had on their lives, is equally important. Often it is not a particular circumstance that determines a character's psychological makeup; rather, it's how she or he *reacts* to the circumstances.

When Sigmund Freud formed his psychological theories, he discovered the tremendous influence that past events have upon our present lives. They shape our actions, our attitudes, and even our fears. Freud saw traumatic events in the past as the cause of the complexes and neuroses of the present. He believed that most abnormal behavior comes from the repression of these events.

The psychologist Carl Jung realized that influences from the past could be a positive source of health, rather than the seeds of mental illness. Sometimes we regain our mental health when we rediscover the values from our childhood.

Many writers use their understanding of childhood influences to help construct a character. Coleman Luck says: "When I was teaching screenwriting there was only one area of psychology that had been extremely important to me— understanding the child of the past. If there is one area that is more important than anything else in applying psychology to writing, it is understanding that the full-blown adult still has the child of the past inside. And if you can understand the child of the past, you can create the critical events of that child's experience that influence your character."

In his studies of childhood, psychoanalyst Erik Erikson found key issues that people must confront at certain ages in order to be healthy, whole, well-adjusted people. As long as these issues remain unresolved, they will continue to exert control over the person's development—at times negatively.

One of the first issues a child confronts is that of trust. An infant needs to feel secure in the world, and this begins with trusting the parents. If this trust is lacking, the child will go through life unable to trust others.

In *Rain Man*, we see both negative and positive events from Charlie's past. Ron Bass tells of these early influences that changed Charlie's ability to trust:

"When Charlie was two years old he lived in a house where his father was a very busy, successful businessman and paid no attention to him at all. But that didn't really register on Charlie because two-year-old Charlie had a loving, caring mother and he had the Rain Man, this brother who was sixteen or eighteen years old, who lived in the house, who never went out, who adored him, and who cuddled him and sang to him.

"But suddenly his mother died, which would be an unbelievably traumatic event for any two-year-old child and especially for a two-year-old boy who was not having a warm, loving relationship with his father. Almost immediately thereafter the only other source of love and comfort he has in the family is sent away and it's a very tearful departure, 'Bye-bye, Rain Man, bye-bye, Rain Man.' So we set up a kid who has all of his emotional supports knocked out from under him at the age of two."

Charlie has a small memory from years ago of this special "Rain Man." When he returns home for his father's funeral, he suddenly thinks of his special friend. He tells Susan:

CHARLIE

I just had this flash of something. You know how when you're a kid . . . you have these sort of . . . pretend friends? Well, mine was named—what the hell was his name? Rain Man. That's it. The

Rain Man. Anyway, if I'd get scared or anything,
I'd just wrap up in this blanket and the Rain Man
would sing to me . . . sing to me by the hour. Now
that I think of it, I must have been scared a lot.
God, that was a long time ago.

SUSAN
So when did he disappear? Your friend?

CHARLIE
I don't know. I just . . . grew up, I guess.

If the child has not found trust as an infant, it will remain an
issue in other relationships throughout one's life. If there is a
change in the stability of a person's life at some later time, the
trust issue may reemerge.

While writing *Gorillas in the Mist*, Anna Hamilton Phelan
felt she needed to understand more about obsessive behavior,
since much of Dian Fossey's behavior seemed obsessive. She
spoke to a psychologist who asked, "Where was she when she
was eleven years old? What was she doing at that age?" When
Anna further researched Dian's biography, she discovered that
her mother had remarried when Dian was that age and that this
marriage had changed the child's ability to trust her world.
"Dian was left alone when she was eleven. I think that's the
first time that she was turned away from people and had to be
by herself. She ate by herself in the kitchen with the help. I
think she was just kind of pushed in the bedroom and kept
pretty much away from her mother and her new stepfather. She
learned to be alone. She learned at that point to mistrust
human beings. She learned to be more comfortable with animals than with people. And she mistrusted human beings
forever—till the day she died."

If in early childhood there is not security, love, and trust,
children will experience an absence of support, and with it a
lack of belief in themselves. Criticism may be substituted for

love in the family. When children enter school, they may either turn the criticism against themselves, becoming rigid, overcontrolled, and rule-oriented, or they may feel ashamed and become defiant, wanting to get even. This rage will be turned either inward ("I'm no good") or outward ("I hate you").

The lack of self-esteem and self-confidence will affect the issue of identity. If children are constantly criticized, their identity is formed by what the parent thinks of them, not by who they really are. The identity issue becomes particularly strong in high school, when teenagers prepare to enter adult life and make adult decisions.

Many teenage films focus on this identity issue. *Risky Business*, *The Karate Kid*, *The Breakfast Club*, and *Pretty in Pink* all deal with young people who are trying to discover their own ideas and feelings, often in contrast to the values and ideas of parents or a conventional/conservative society.

Erikson says that children with a healthy background are more likely to become autonomous. If the opposite is true, the child (and later the adult) will be less free to make decisions for fear of being criticized or rejected.

In *Rain Man*, the key issue in the years to follow was Charlie's desire for his father's affection. Throughout his early years, Charlie was "overcontrolled," trying to please his father in order to win his father's love.

Ron Bass says, "The father's response to Raymond—the abnormal child—was to lock him away and treat him like some kind of freak who didn't deserve to be treated normally. But he treated his normal child in much the same way. Nothing that Charlie did was ever good enough. Charlie couldn't be perfect. The father had one son who was imperfect, who was autistic, so the second son had to be perfect and fill his life—and his second son wasn't perfect. True, he was terrific—he got good grades, he was handsome, but that wasn't good enough. Nothing he could do was ever good enough because Charlie's father felt that the world had owed him some kind of perfection.

"I don't think that Charlie was a rebel at all when he was

younger. Because he so instinctively felt the need for his father's love and affection, the less love the father gave him, the
more Charlie craved it. So I think that Charlie spent his childhood busting his butt to be perfect for his father. And nothing
was ever good enough."

When Charlie was sixteen, he had one moment of
rebellion—to test whether his father would still love him, even
if he were "bad." Charlie discusses this moment with his girl-
friend, Susan.

CHARLIE

Tell you one story. Just one. Y'know that convert-
ible out front . . . ? His baby. That and the goddam
roses. Car was off-limits to me. That's a classic,
he'd say. It commands respect. Not for children.
Tenth grade. I'm sixteen. And for once . . . I bring
home a report card . . . and it's all A's. . . . So I go
to my dad. Can I take the guys out in the Buick?
Sort of a victory drive. He says no. But I go anyway. Steal the keys. Sneak it out.

SUSAN

Why then? Why that time?

CHARLIE

Because I deserved it. I'd done something wonderful. In his own terms. And he wasn't man
enough to do right. So we're on Lakeshore Drive.
Four kids. Four six-packs. And we get pulled over.
He'd called in a report of a stolen car. Not his
son took the car without permission. Just . . .
stolen.
    (beat)
Cook County Jail. Other guys' dads bail 'em out
in an hour. He left me there. Two . . . days.

[69]

Drunks throwing up. Psychos all over me. Some
guy tries to rape me. Twice. That's the only time
in my life . . . I was gut-scared. Shit-your-pants
. . . heart-pounding-right-through-your-ribs . . .
can't-catch-your-breath scared. The guy knifed
my back . . . that's the . . .

SUSAN

. . . scar. By your shoulder.

CHARLIE

I left home. I never came back.

With this incident, Charlie learned the truth—that his father didn't love him.

Ron explains, "And so he defies his father and deliberately
makes a very clean break in his life. This is a central moment in
his life—at sixteen when he walks away out of his father's life
forever. And in doing this, he gave up on all the things that he
worked hard to achieve—such as college. Charlie is a bright
guy, he's a guy who could have been a young yuppie executive
somewhere, but he had to rebel against his father and strike
back at his father by denying him the pleasure of vicarious
success that he knows his father wanted. And in the process of
rebelling against his father, he destroyed his own life.

"So what do you say to yourself when you're bright and you
want the finer things of life? Your father is successful, and a
millionaire, and you've spent sixteen years chasing that, and so
it's not like you've always wanted to rebel against that. All along
you've always wanted to achieve that and make your dad proud
of you. So what do you say when you walk away from that? You
can't say that you're deliberately destroying yourself to hurt
your father—people don't realize that at that level—instead
you say, 'My father's a fool, and what I thought I wanted all my
life was shallow and materialistic and false and who needs to
take that robotic path to success? I'm better than my father

ever was and I'll do it fast and easy and cheap. I'll go out with only myself to rely on—I can do it!'

"And that's what he went out to do and that's when he became a hustler. He was smart, and this car business that we see him in is probably only the last in a long line of things. He's not in the gutter, he's not broke, because he's so darn smart that even doing it the wrong way he's been able to have modest successes. But Charlie's a guy who wants to fail. He's always believed in the back of his mind that his father was right. So as much as he hates his father on the surface, he knows somewhere deep down in his heart his father is right, and when his father says he's a loser he must really be a loser."

This lack of trust in childhood prevented Charlie Babbitt from being able to love as an adult.

Erikson says that adulthood is a time to resolve the issues of intimacy versus isolation—to learn to relate closely to each other in order to form marriages and friendships and alliances. If these issues have not been resolved—problems of mistrust, doubt, guilt, can all come into a relationship, impeding the potential to be intimate.

"Charlie is in an uncommitted relationship with Susan," Ron Bass continues, "with someone he doesn't have to worry about hurting because she can take care of herself. She's not asking him to marry her; she's cool. She's as able to leave him as he's able to leave her and that's a real Charlie Babbitt relationship that doesn't demand commitment or anything real. He's smiling. He's charming. He's got her convinced that he really cares about her and that's all she's asked for. But if it hadn't been for Raymond, he could have lost that woman two months earlier and he wouldn't have missed her. It's the change that starts to occur in him as he goes on the road. As he begins to change, he realizes what a terrific lady he lost, and how much he didn't want to lose her. He calls, and that melts her because she had never seen him that way."

It is Charlie's transformation that helps him reconnect with the positive influence from his past—his brother. In one of the beautiful surprises in the film, Charlie discovers that Raymond had been his childhood playmate, and that there had been a healthy emotional tie between them.

In fact, this transformation is what the story is about. Ron says, "The hope is that you walk out of the theatre feeling that Charlie will be able to love Susan and others and to have children and to join the world of caring people because of what he's learned about himself through his experience with his brother."

If these issues had not been resolved with Charlie, he would have reached another crisis—the crisis Erik Erikson calls "generativity versus stagnation." This occurs when a person has not lived up to his or her talents. Sometimes this becomes the mid-life crisis, where people have to confront where they've come in their lives, and what they've accomplished.

When someone reaches forty and fifty and beyond, there is another crisis, one of "integrity versus despair." This crisis is not just one of accomplishments and professional contributions, but of meaning and value. At this point, people confront whether their lives mean anything, whether they've had depth. The consequences of not resolving these issues can lead to despair, alcoholism, depression, even suicide. *The Verdict* and *Who Framed Roger Rabbit?*—despite the broad differences in their genres—were both about resolving issues from the past, confronting a crisis in the present, and learning to become involved and caring as a result.

EXERCISE: Imagine creating a story about a future Charlie Babbitt. What might he be like if you set the story at his mid-life crisis, when Charlie is about forty and still failing because he unconsciously felt his father was correct about his inability to succeed? What might Charlie do to compensate?

What would Charlie be like if he were sixty, trying to find meaning in life while still being controlled by his father? How might he express his despair?

What might he be like at these stages if he had resolved his mid-life crisis? What would you expect his relationship with his brother to be like, if the film continued into the future?

HOW THE UNCONSCIOUS DETERMINES CHARACTER

Many psychologists believe that our conscious awareness makes up only about ten percent of the human psyche. What drives and motivates us comes more from the unconscious, which consists of feelings, memories, experiences, and impressions that have been imprinting our minds from birth. These elements, which are often repressed because of negative associations, drive our behavior, causing us to act in ways that might contradict our conscious belief systems or our own understanding of ourselves.

Many elements in our lives, although not known to our conscious minds, drive our behavior. These forces can cause us to act in ways that contradict our belief systems or our own identities.

We have all had conversations with people who come across as though they understand themselves. But as we listen to them, we sense that their impression of themselves is quite different from the one we have of them. A woman may tell us what an open person she is, when in truth she's defensive, resistant, closed. A man may appear gentle, but later betray a violent nature that even he may not have known was there. Some of these people may be driven by an unconscious drive for power, or a desire to control, or by maliciousness or cruelty.

People usually have little knowledge of how these unconscious forces influence their behavior. Often these are negative elements that are denied or rationalized. Psychologists call this "the shadow" or the "dark side of the personality."

We've seen a number of examples in the news of the unconscious shadow operating in people's lives. Jimmy Swaggart is a "moralist" who was brought down by his "denied sexuality." Nixon, a president for "law and order," was brought down by the illegalities committed by his administration.

Within the shadow side of the unconscious can be found rage, sexuality, depression—or, to define it in another way, the seven deadly sins of anger, gluttony, sloth, pride, envy, avarice, and lust.

These unconscious forces achieve more power when they are repressed or denied. Unacknowledged, they can drive people to do and say things against their will. Suppressed, they have more potential to get people into trouble.

Sometimes writers decide that this shadow side is the side that they want to explore. Barry Morrow says: "My stories *Bill* and *Bill on His Own* explored the positive human aspects. I wanted *Rain Man* to be about the opposite—the darker side of human motivation, about greed and avarice, and shortsightedness and impatience. Charlie is the dark side of me—the dark side of everybody. I had a feeling that Mother Theresa gets angry every once in a while. I'll bet the Pope gets awfully impatient with some of the bowing and scraping. I know everybody has both the good and the bad, the light and the dark, the yin and the yang inside of them, and *Bill* was all about the light and the hopefulness, and *Rain Man* was about the opposite."

Exploring the dark side doesn't mean that your story ends on a negative note. "I challenged myself," Barry says, "to believe that the story would end up the same way—a sense of making human connections and about piecing back together your life and winnowing out the pain and going on."

Charlie has no recognition that his actions and behavior are driven, to a great extent, by his need for his father's love and approval. According to Ron Bass, "Charlie's need is to be self-contained, to keep himself walled off from feeling the hurt of rejection. What drives Charlie is wanting his father's love, knowing he won't get it, knowing that his father might be right and that he's going to fail. The biggest problems in our lives are the ones we're always redoing, hoping that it will be different the next time, that we'll get it right. His biggest goal is to prove his father wrong, and yet deep down in his heart he keeps proving his father right. He could prove his father wrong by being a success, on his own terms in his own way, without his father's help or guidance. That would prove that he doesn't need his father's love."

The unconscious manifests itself in your characters through their behavior, gestures, and speech. All these underlying drives and meanings that are unknown to the characters will nevertheless affect what they say and do.

HOW PERSONALITY DIFFERENCES CREATE CHARACTER

Although we may all be of the same human species, we are not all the same types of people. Each of us experiences life in different ways. We have varied outlooks and perceptions about life.

Writers throughout the centuries have used an understanding of character types to help draw the broad strokes of their characters.

In the Middle Ages and the Renaissance, writers believed that the physical body could be divided into four elements, or humors, just as the physical world was divided into the four elements of earth, air, fire, and water. These humors included black bile, blood, yellow bile, and phlegm. One's temperament (or character type) was determined by the predominance of one humor.

The personality controlled by black bile was melancholic— thoughtful, sentimental, affected, unenterprising. Hamlet's gloomy indecisions and Jacques's brooding in *As You Like It* are instances of the melancholy temperament.

A personality dominated by blood would be sanguine— beneficent, joyful, amorous. Falstaff would fit this temperament.

[75]

The choleric personality, dominated by yellow bile, is easily angered, impatient, obstinate, and vengeful. Both Othello's jealousy and Lear's rashness show an extreme of choler.

And the phlegmatic personality is composed, undemonstrative, with a coolness and calm fortitude; for example, Horatio in *Hamlet*.

The perfect temperament is one in which all four humors are perfectly balanced. Conversely, a serious imbalance could produce maladjustment, craziness.

Brutus in *Julius Caesar* possessed a nearly ideal balance. Marc Antony called him "the noblest Roman of them all":

> *. . . the elements*
> *So mixed in him that Nature might stand up*
> *And say to all the world, "This was a man!"*

Ian Fleming, in *Octopussy*, updates these four elements in his description of a drunk. "The sanguine drunk goes gay to the point of hysteria and idiocy; the phlegmatic sinks into a morass of sullen gloom; the choleric is the fighting drunk of the cartoonists who spends much of his life in prison for smashing people and things; and the melancholic succumbs to self-pity, mawkishness, and tears."[1]

Shakespeare was interested in the relationships between characters. Some types get along well because they see the world in compatible ways. But other relationships cause conflict. For instance, someone who is choleric—who demands quick actions and responses—will be driven crazy by someone who is phlegmatic and wants to think things out. Someone who is sanguine will find it depressing to be around the melancholic.

During the last hundred years, there has been much reinterpretation of these personality types, and, as a writer, being familiar with the theories can be helpful in differentiating your characters, and strengthening character conflicts.

Carl Jung says that most people tend toward either extraversion or introversion. Social extraverts focus on the outside world, and introverts focus on an inner reality. Extraverts tend to be comfortable in crowds, easily relate to others, love parties and people. Introverts are loners, pursuing solitary activities such as reading or meditation. They look within rather than without for the center of their lives.

In drama, as in real life, most characters are extraverts. Extraverts move the action, and provide the conflict and the dynamic of the film. They are outer-directed people who function well with others and who actively interact with life. But *Rain Man* proved that an introvert could make a powerful character, when paired with a more active character to move the action.

Ron Bass says, "Raymond is most certainly an introvert. The classical autistic doesn't understand other people as being that different from trees or inanimate objects. He doesn't understand that people are people.

"Charlie is an introvert in extravert clothing. Charlie feels comfortable in a crowd because he feels he can manage it. He's gorgeous and charming, but I don't think he derives any real joy or fun from being in a crowd. He's always thinking behind his eyes, What do they want from me, what do I want from them? He's a kind of a loner in the sense that his true feelings are never shared. He is so walled off. His anger is at the surface, and he's talkative and he's aggressive and he's a take-charge guy, but he can't share his true feelings, they're hidden from himself as well as from others."

Carl Jung added four other categories to the introvert and extravert to further the understanding of personality types: the sensation type, the thinking type, the feeling type, and the intuitive type.

Sensation people experience life through the senses. They are attuned to their physical environment—to colors and smells, shapes and tastes. They tend to live in the present, responding to the things around them. Many sensation types make good cooks, house builders, doctors, photographers—any occupation that is physical and sensory-oriented. James

Bond would probably be considered a sensation type—sensual, a lover of fast cars, physical activities, and beautiful women.

Thinking types are the opposite. They think through a situation, figure out the problem, and take control to bring about a solution. They make decisions based on principles, not on feelings. They're logical, objective, methodical. Thinking types tend to make good administrators, engineers, mechanics, executives. Characters who have strong thinking functions include Perry Mason, Jessica Fletcher, MacGyver, and the Marquise in *Dangerous Liaisons*.

Feeling types have a sense of rapport with others. They care, are sympathetic and warmhearted. Their feelings are often accessible and up front. Teachers, social workers, and nurses are often feeling types. In films and novels, they would include Madame de Torville in *Dangerous Liaisons*, Pfc. Eriksson in *Casualties of War*, Tess McGill in *Working Girl*.

Intuitives are interested in future possibilities. They're the dreamers, with new visions, plans, ideas. They play hunches, have premonitions, and live in anticipation of what will come to pass in the future. Intuitives are often entrepreneurs, inventors, and artists whose ideas sometimes come to them "full-blown." Some bank robbers and gamblers are intuitives, looking to future enjoyment of their wealth. Obi-Wan-Kenobi from *Star Wars* is an intuitive who recognizes the nature of the invisible Force. Sam in "Cheers" is also an intuitive—he always has a hunch that he's going to get any woman he wants. Even Gordon Gekko in *Wall Street* seems to have a strong intuitive function as he plans and schemes.

These functions never exist alone. Most people have two dominant functions and two inferior functions (sometimes called the "shadow functions"). Most people—and most characters—will tend to gain their information about the world around them either through sensation (direct experience) or through intuition. And they will tend to process information either through thinking or through feeling.

"Charlie is a thinker and an intuitive," Ron Bass says. "He's probably one of those people who lives by the past and the future. In spite of the fact that he might seem to be a guy who lived hedonistically in the moment, he's really driven by the ghosts of the past and he's fueled by his dreams that someday he'll strike it rich and he'll hit the jackpot. So he gets himself in these messes—settling past debts by gambling on the future glories. I'm not sure that he lives for the moment."

An understanding of these categories can be useful to create characters who don't look and act alike, and to help you to create dynamic character relationships.

People frequently have the greatest conflict with their opposite. The sensation detective may have trouble with the intuitive who plays hunches not based on solid evidence. The thinker may dislike the feeling type who seems overly sentimental and ignores the facts.

Others idolize the person who expresses their weakest function. If people are weak in intuition, they may seek out the intuitive guru who will take over that function for them. If they're weak in thinking, they may seek out the idea person. Nonfeeling types might turn to a passionate, moralistic preacher to carry their feeling for them. Women who are weak in sensation are particularly vulnerable to the ladies' man, or to the passionate love affair.

Depending on the particular story you want to tell, you may find that other ways of defining character types can be helpful. In the book *The Hero Within*, Carol Pearson describes the "six archetypes we live by" as the orphan, the innocent, the wanderer, the martyr, the warrior, and the magician. Mark Gerzon, in *A Choice of Heroes*, discusses several male character types, such as the soldier, the frontiersman, the nurturer. Jean Shinoda-Bolen, in her books, *Goddesses in Every Woman* and *Gods in Every Man*, uses god and goddess images to help understand human nature. Any of these books can be helpful for expanding individual characters and understanding differences between characters.

EXERCISE: Writing is an act of inner exploration. Many of the writers interviewed for this book say that each character is, to some extent, an aspect of themselves. Think about what character type you identify with—thinking, intuition, sensation, feeling. Imagine responding to life as your opposite. If you're a sensation type, imagine being intuitive. If you're a thinking type, imagine life as a feeling type. How does the emphasis of each of these qualities change your personality? Think about your acquaintances. What character types do you think they are? How are they different from you?

HOW ABNORMAL BEHAVIOR DEFINES CHARACTER

I'm sure you know the old saying, "All of us are a little bit crazy, and thee more than me." Most psychologists recognize that the line between normal and abnormal is not a clear-cut one.

If you are writing a script about an abnormal personality, whether about a schizophrenic, a manic-depressive, a paranoid, or a psychotic, you will need to do a great deal of specific research about the complexities of these personality disorders.

In order to create the character of Raymond Babbitt, Barry Morrow needed to know the characteristics of the autistic, the autistic savant, and the mentally retarded. Barry relates how he became interested in the autistic savant: "I had volunteered some time every year to the Association for Retarded Citizens. One afternoon we were having a break and I felt a tap on my shoulder and there—one-half inch from my nose—was the nose of Rain Man. Kim is his name. And he cocked his head with a sort of quizzical look on his face and said to me, 'Think about it, Barry Morrow.' And I took a good yard step back and cocked my head and thought about what he had said; and he looked sort of like a Zen master in his own peculiar way, and, mercifully, just then his father showed up to make sense of it all. He introduced me to Kim and he said that Kim was so excited to meet me that that's why he got his words mixed up. What he meant to say was 'I think about you, Barry Morrow.' And he turned his head the other way and started making this groaning sound and started flapping his hands real fast, and then he started to say some names.

"I didn't know what was going on, but then I recognized one name that seemed familiar, and then another, and I realized that what he was doing was reciting the names from the credits from my movies, *Bill* and *Bill on His Own*—in order. Then he started again with numbers, but they were going by so fast they made no sense. And his father asked Kim to slow down and told him that I didn't understand. He slowed down and I realized he was giving my phone numbers of the last eight or ten years over and over again. His father said he memorizes phone books for a hobby—thousands. He generally only memorizes the Yellow Pages but in my case he made an exception. Anything he reads he commits to memory. The more questions I asked, the more astounded I was by the answers, and there seemed to be no end to the amazing aspects of this person. I flew home and my head was just spinning with him. I just knew I had met one of the world's extraordinary creatures and how privileged I was."

Whereas Kim was the original model for Raymond, Dustin Hoffman chose a different model for Raymond, according to Ron Bass.

"Dustin did a tremendous amount of research on the classically autistic personality. He modeled his character after a very particular guy. This person had a brother who was not autistic, so we sat with the brother a great deal. He would imitate his autistic brother and I began to get a rhythm of who the guy was. I needed to find ways in which the guy would do things that were quirky and autistic but somehow were charming rather than off-putting. That's why we used the notion of keeping the personal injury list—it's universal, since we all do it ourselves to some extent. It's very personally relatable. We added the rituals—you can have rituals that are obnoxious and very distasteful, but you can also have rituals that are very adorable. With only two hours for a movie, we chose what was charming and interesting rather than off-putting."

Understanding abnormal behavior is essential when writing these kinds of characters. But having some knowledge about abnormal behavior can also be helpful when writing about normal characters. All of us have some of these elements within us. Giving your normal characters some of these characteristics can add conflict and interest.

David Williamson, the Australian writer of *Gallipoli* and *Phar Lapp,* has a master's degree in psychology. He finds it useful to think of his characters in terms of clinical abnormal personality models. Although this is not how he creates them, he often returns to this model during the rewrite phase, pushing his characters slightly off the normal line in order to create more drama and more interest.

Clinical psychology identifies a number of personality or temperament types that are seen as hindering the person's psychological functioning. Williamson diagrams them in this way:

EXTRAVERTED

| | | Psychopath |
Manic	Paranoid	or sociopath

| Normal behavior line | | |
| Depressive | Schizophrenic | Anxiety neurotic |

INTROVERTED

As with personality types, a character with an abnormal personality does not always fall completely in one category. Manic-depressives fluctuate between the two, as do paranoid-schizophrenics. You might draw upon these categories for broad strokes and consistency in creating normal characters, as well as to create strong dynamics between characters.

Manic types think they can do anything. They appear very optimistic, exhibiting a kind of emotional euphoria. Highly excitable and often very social, manics are easily given to emotional outbursts. They can be frivolous and overtalkative. Their attention span is short and their threshold for boredom extremely low. Furthermore, as they pursue what they want, they tend to trample on others with little thought.

Characters who are normal, but have some manic qualities, may be workaholics, driven by the need to succeed. They may be driven by greed, as is Gordon Gekko in *Wall Street*, or by a belief that everything will work out and they can build a whole new world, as is Allie in *The Mosquito Coast*, or by a conviction that they can do anything, as are the villains in *Superman*.

Charlie Babbitt is a bit manic at times. Ron Bass says, "Charlie is very frenetic. He's too defensive, too self-controlled to get really depressed. I don't think Charlie is a guy that ever sat around and moped."

Depressives are the other side of the coin. They tend to conserve their emotional energy. They are subject to black moods, feelings of worthlessness and inferiority. Some tend to be hypochondriacs, or to blame themselves even when they are not at fault. Characters who might be considered normal, but contain a number of these qualities are: Hamlet, Martin Riggs in *Lethal Weapon*, and David from the play *Strange Snow* (later made into the film *Jackknife*).

Schizophrenic characters have appeared in a number of successful films. *I Never Promised You a Rose Garden*, *David and Lisa*, and the television movie *Promise* all come to mind. Schizophrenics tend to be shy, self-conscious, overly sensitive, and easily embarrassed. They protect their ego by avoiding open conflict. They withdraw, sulk, and generally have a difficult time communicating. Arthur "Boo" Radley in *To Kill a Mockingbird* might be considered borderline schizophrenic, and Macon in *The Accidental Tourist* could be considered a normal personality with some schizophrenic characteristics, brought on by his grief over the death of his son.

Paranoids believe people are out to get them. As a result, they tend to be aggressive. They want to be leaders, to have power and prestige over others. They are decisive, stubborn, opinionated, defensive, often competitive, arrogant, conceited, and boastful. They often harbor unreasonable grudges, are quick to take offense, and are very sensitive to any personal criticism, which supports their belief that others don't like them. Many of the Charles Bronson and Sylvester Stallone film characters show some of these qualities.

Anxiety neurotics worry about and fear everything. They are concerned about personal safety, terror-stricken about the greenhouse effect, the ozone layer, acid rain, rape, and the general realities of life. For them, disaster lurks everywhere. They spend their lives trying to avoid anxiety. The favorite anxiety neurotic for many moviegoers is Woody Allen, in such films as *Hannah and Her Sisters, Annie Hall*, and *Zelig*.

The obsessive/compulsive character also is a neurotic. Alex's obsession with the unwilling Dan in *Fatal Attraction* and the compulsion of Raymond Babbitt, who has to watch "People's Court" every day, are both examples of obsessive behavior that drives the character.

We see the sociopath (who is antisocial) or psychopath (who is also mentally unbalanced) in many films, as well as in the daily newspapers. These are often the villains in a story, the "hardened criminals," the people with no moral center who can be fearless, untrustworthy, out for their own personal gain and self-preservation, with no empathy for others. As an antagonist, a sociopath or psychopath will go to any lengths to impede the good intentions of the protagonist.

These characters do not transform. If you decide to have characters who are psychopaths or sociopaths, remember that they cannot become normal, well-adjusted individuals by the end of the film.

Almost all of the famous Edward G. Robinson and James Cagney films, such as *White Heat, Little Caesar,* and *Scarface,* focus on the sociopath. The sociopath also appears in *The Godfather, Helter Skelter,* and *Bonnie and Clyde.*

Drama and conflict can come from the relationship between these characters. Paranoids need someone to persecute them, and will find the manic's aggressiveness a threat. The manic finds the depressive's lack of energy and drive a frustration. The psychopath has no understanding of the anxiety neurotic's fears.

If you are writing an abnormal character, you will probably need to do additional psychological research. Reading medical journals and psychology books, talking to psychologists, perhaps even meeting or observing people with an abnormal personality disorder will all be helpful.

Although this material may seem clinical, thinking of your characters as having some abnormal tendencies can add conflict and complexity. Some writers try to make their characters too nice, too likable, too sane—thereby destroying any edge that might make them interesting. Looking at these categories can help you round out your characters, recognizing that even nice characters may have a little craziness in them.

Barry Morrow says: "Whether you make a formal study of psychology, or whether you learn it by being in the world and being observant of human behavior, you need to have a deep enough well to write from. You have to have had the opportunity of being bounced around enough in this world by strange people, in order to understand human behavior."

Novelist Dennis Lynds concurs: "The person who becomes a writer is undoubtedly already interested in the psychology and sociology of character. Just as a painter had better be interested in color or he's not going to be very much of a painter, we as writers have to be interested in psychology."

James Dearden adds: "We don't go out and learn psychology as we're writing the character. You probably hope that you have a sense of how people tick, but any psychology you learn, you try to learn in a general, not a specific way. You're not there to study psychology because you're creating this specific character. Hopefully you already have a general sense of psychology, which enables you to create characters. We all have psychological knowledge on the most elemental level. We may not have fancy names for why we do things or why other people do things, but we all know that if you brutalize a child, chances are that child will brutalize when he gets older. You don't have to be a genius to figure that one out. These are part of one's experience. I think that's why in the end I keep coming back to knowing oneself. If you know yourself you can know other people. Until you know yourself, you can't know other people."

A CASE STUDY:
ORDINARY PEOPLE

Ordinary People is a psychological novel, about a boy tormented by guilt over the death of his brother. It's a novel about identity, transformation, and change. The film version, written by Alvin Sargent, won several Academy Awards. For the purposes of this book, we will be dealing with the novel, although readers may want to watch the film to see how this psychological information was adapted to the screen.

Novelist Judith Guest approaches psychology from an understanding of her own experience, by reaching inside herself to get to the core of a character.

"Although I only took one psychology class in college, I collect news articles and I read a great many books on psychology. I haven't read a great deal of Jung's work, but I decided the Jungian theory is the theory I'm most closely aligned to.

"So much of what I do to understand psychology is unconscious research. I'm like a sponge absorbing all kinds of information from every direction I turn, yet I'm not always aware that that's what I'm doing. But because it's a subject that interests me, my ears, eyes, paws are wide open for it all the time."

Judith's work on the psychology of her characters includes understanding their behavior, their relationships to each other, and their potential to be transformed. Most of the strokes she gives her characters come out of her intuitive understanding of why people act the way they do.

Notice that when she talks about her characters, she talks about their *inner* workings. It's not so much their outer behavior that interests her as how they think, how they see the world, the relationship between their inner and outer realities.

"With most of the characters I was going on my gut feeling of what they would be like. When I developed Burger, I wanted to create a psychiatrist that would be the best kind of psychiatrist for Conrad [the suicidal son]. I thought, What kind of guy would this be? He'd have to be as smart as this kid and have a pretty good sense of humor, because that's Conrad's way of combating the world. And I wanted a guy that uses the same method of dealing with the world through humor, but uses it more constructively than his patient. I wanted a man who was able to look at life in a lighthearted way. Not to be able to push away the reality of life and discount his feelings of what's happening in life.

"Beth [the mother] is like a number of people I've known. With her I was trying to create a character who had been desperately hurt and her only way to deal with it was to deny and become more and more remote from the realities of her existence. She was afraid of her own emotions and of dealing with them. I think she was afraid if she ever faced the situation she would totally fall apart. This was her way of holding herself together, which makes her not different from a lot of other people in the world."

Some of the inner workings of Judith Guest's characters she learns as she writes about them. For instance, her attitude toward Beth changed, the more she observed her. "I think

[87]

when I first started writing Beth, I hated her. I blamed her for what had happened to Conrad. The longer I wrote, the more complex the situation appeared to me and the less I blamed her. She was the way she was. He was also the way he was and he learned to be different and she didn't. She wasn't able to rise above the situation."

For a novelist, communicating character psychology leaves open the possibility of getting inside the head of the character—of letting the reader know what the character is feeling and thinking. With the characters of Calvin (the father) and Conrad, Judith chose to do so. With Beth, she made a conscious choice not to.

"I didn't think that understanding Conrad's or Calvin's character would be that difficult. So I went inside both their heads, and chose not to go inside Beth's because I felt it would be too difficult to try. The truth is: I didn't understand her character. I know there are people like this and there are reasons why they are the way they are, but to get inside her head and try to portray what they were seemed very difficult to me."

Judith needed to understand the relationship and transforming potential of one person for another—and how that would change what was going on inside their heads. I asked Judith if she thought Beth was transformable. "Definitely. I think a lot of it is timing. What happened in that family was that two people were ready and one person was not. And when that happens you have a choice. That is to hang in there and be ready, or to leave; and she opted to leave.

"Calvin was able to be transformed because Calvin was a less defensive person. And his defenses were washed away by the event of Conrad trying to commit suicide, and his main determination was, it was not going to happen again and he was going to do everything to make sure it didn't. Calvin realized that Conrad's suicide attempt came from not being able to talk over his feelings with other people and if he had to sit on the kid's doorstep and bug him about it every day of his life, he was not going to let that happen again.

[88]

"I really see Conrad and his mother being more alike than he and his father. I think it's the thing that kept them apart. They were both afraid of life and they kept life at a distance. They both were real perfectionists. So this real failure in their life—Buck [Conrad's brother] being drowned and lost—was more than either one of them could bear. Perfectionists also are guilt-ridden and Conrad was extremely guilt-ridden even though it wasn't his fault. He took her avoidance of dealing with anything as more evidence that he was guilty. I don't think she hated him or blamed him for the accident. I think it was more that neither one of them was able to deal with the grief of this and they buried it and it leaks out in all these other ways. When Conrad tried to let go of these destructive behaviors in his life, he couldn't tolerate them any more in his mother.

"I think Conrad's way of dealing with things was always to joke about it and slough them off. Rather than confronting the hostility he encounters from Stillman [the jock] he makes some crack back, which doesn't resolve anything. To me it was a measure of his mental health when he finally got in a big fight with him. He had had it with Stillman. It was a very direct reaction."

The movement in *Ordinary People* is a movement toward both mental health and transformation for Conrad and Calvin, as well as one toward finding meaning in life. "There are things in people's lives that just defy meaning," Judith Guest says. "You can go crazy trying to figure out what the meaning of something is. When Conrad says to Burger in their final scene, 'Don't you see, it's got to be somebody's fault or what was the whole point of it?' Burger says, 'There was no point, it happened. It is true that people search for meaning, but the search for meaning can hang you up if there's a terrible tragedy.'

"Both Calvin and Conrad formed a stronger identity. By the end of the book, they're certainly more expanded people, deeper people, more relational, more feeling—they care more, and I think they're trying to be more honest. They began to get in touch with that core person of who they really are—

and they stop being judgmental. Something good did come of all this!"

APPLICATION

Knowing the inner workings of your character can help create a stronger and more understandable character. To begin with, ask yourself:

- What traumatic incidents in my character's past might affect present behavior? Are there good influences in the past that might influence transformation in the present?
- What unconscious forces are driving my character? How do they affect my character's motivations, actions, and goals?
- What character types have I drawn upon for my major and supporting characters? Am I getting contrast and conflict from these character relationships?
- Have I made my characters too nice, too bland, too normal? Is there anything a little abnormal about them? How do their abnormalities cause conflict with other characters?

SUMMARY

People are always more than systems. Yet there are certain consistent patterns of behavior and attitudes that are governed by their psychology. Understanding that people are both the same in terms of certain basic desires and different in terms of how they respond to life can be a key to creating dimensional characters with both a rich outer life and a rich inner one.

5

Creating
Character Relationships

Characters rarely exist alone—they exist in relationships. Aside from an occasional one-character story (for instance, *Krapp's Last Tape,* by Samuel Beckett, or *Duel,* by Steven Spielberg), most stories are about the interaction between people. For many films and television series, the dynamic between the characters can be as important as any individual character quality.

Novelist Leonard Tourney emphasizes the change in focus in the twentieth century. "Couples have become increasingly important in fiction and film. There are innumerable stories with partners—police partners, husband-and-wife teams. It introduces into the story a kind of chemistry, creates a new person, a new identity, something new. When you put any two people or objects together, you have a new thing. People as couples are different from the individual. It's not conscious, but couples tend to behave differently when they're together."

Some of the most successful films and television series have featured two stars, not one. A partial list of relational television series would include "Cheers," "Kate and Allie," "Moonlighting," "Mork and Mindy," "Starsky and Hutch," "Cagney and

Lacey," and "Remington Steele." Many successful films also emphasize character relationships. Think of *The African Queen, Butch Cassidy and the Sundance Kid, Adam's Rib, 48 HRS., Lethal Weapon,* and *Rain Man.*

Relational stories emphasize the chemistry between characters. The individual characters are created by choosing qualities that will provide the most "sizzle" in the relationship. The most sizzle comes from a combination of the following elements:

1. Characters have something in common that brings them together and keeps them together. This is the attraction between the characters.
2. There is a conflict between the characters that threatens to pull them apart and that provides much of the drama—and sometimes the comedy—in a script.
3. Characters have contrasting qualities; they are opposites. This creates new conflicts and strengthens the characters through opposition.
4. The characters have the potential to transform each other—for better or for worse.

HOW DO YOU BALANCE ATTRACTION AND CONFLICT?

Conflict is an essential element in almost all fiction writing. Most stories rely on conflict to provide tension and interest and drama to the story. But many stories are also love stories— portraying the attraction between people. In films and novels it is relatively easy to find the balance between conflict and attraction. Conflict begins the story but gets resolved at the end, usually leading to the happy ending.

But the television series presents a special problem. A series may run for five to ten years, delaying the resolution of the relationship. If the attraction overcomes the conflict, and the characters come together too soon, the sizzle can leave the show. If there's too much conflict, and too little attraction, characters can become unlikable, and audiences will tune them out. This is further complicated because it's unnatural to keep characters apart, particularly when the strength of the series depends on the characters' mutual interest. Finding this balance becomes a challenge for producers and writers.

James Burrows (cocreator of "Cheers") explains how they dealt with this dilemma at the beginning of the series: "Our show is an evolving show. And the critics were not crazy about Diane and Sam's evolution. We felt if Sam and Diane stayed in the teasing stage it would invalidate Sam's character. You can only keep Diane and Sam apart for so long. Obviously, if he's a ladies' man, he has to score with Diane eventually, or he's not a very successful ladies' man. We liked what this coming together did for the characters and the new definition it gave us, and we liked breaking them up again."

In shows such as "Who's the Boss?," "Moonlighting," and "Cheers," the attraction, even the friendship, between these characters is real. It's clear that they genuinely like each other on many levels. In a joint interview, Marty Cohan and Blake Hunter, creators of "Who's the Boss?," describe some of the commonality between Angela and Tony:

"Both Tony and Angela are conservative, in terms of how they look at life. They're very basic people—conscious of family and home. They would rather sit at home and watch TV and eat popcorn than go out on the town. They're very supportive of each other."

The repartee between Maddie and David on "Moonlighting"—and their fantasies of each other—reveal feelings that they usually are unable to express directly. In this scene, from the script of "It's a Wonderful Job" by Carl Sautter and Debra Frank, Maddie is a ghost, seeing what life would have been like if she had closed the agency two years ago. Albert is her guardian angel, taking her through this experience. David is ready to marry Cheryl Tiegs, yet he can't get Maddie out of his mind. Although David can't hear or see her, she responds to his musings.

> DAVID
> I was just thinking . . . Maddie Hayes . . . That was a name I hadn't heard for a while. She slapped me once. She was even a great slapper. . . . There was something . . . she had class, strength. I really admired her.

> MADDIE
> You did?

> DAVID
> She had this softness about her, this warmth. It was just a feeling. I bet she was a really special girl.

> MADDIE
> Oh, David. What does he mean, was?

> DAVID
> Maybe, we could have been great together.

> MADDIE
> But we were great together . . . don't you remember all those cases? The disc jockey, the piano player, that stupid portrait of me. You followed me to Buenos Aires . . . I followed you to New York. How could you forget that? You even kissed me once in a garage.

> ALBERT
> No, he didn't, Maddie.

> MADDIE
> What?

ALBERT
None of that happened.

MADDIE
Huh?

ALBERT
All that went away when you closed the agency.
Those two years, they're gone.

DAVID
Ah, this is crazy. Here I am comparing Cheryl to a
woman I don't even know.

In another situation, this attraction would be the focus of
the show, and you might see a 1950s love story where the
characters fall in love, get married, and have babies. But in
order to keep the characters apart in a credible way, barriers
are created. Usually the barrier comes from the situation—
such as a working relationship. Whether this relationship is a
working partnership (as in "Moonlighting"), or an employer-
employee relationship (as in "Cheers" or "Who's the Boss?"),
the barrier works because at least one character recognizes the
problems that can occur by mixing business and pleasure.

Constructing the barrier can be difficult. It needs to be
weak enough so that a great deal of love and affection can flow
back and forth, but strong enough so at least one character
understands the value of not giving in. In "Who's the Boss?"
both characters have that same value. They might be attracted
to each other, but as long as they live in the same house with
the children, they won't sleep together. In "Cheers," Diane
(and later Rebecca) is doubly determined not to give in to Sam's
amorous advances.

In these series, the barrier is always toyed with. Usually the
titillation comes from playing with these boundaries, although
if there's too much toying with them, audiences might question

the indecisiveness of the characters. On the other hand, if there is none, audiences might question why two attractive people are so uninterested in each other.

Both "Moonlighting" and "Cheers" eventually crossed the line. David and Maddie, and Diane and Sam, eventually slept together.

In 1985, in its third year, "Who's the Boss?" toyed with the boundary, and reaffirmed the balance:

> ANGELA
> Nothing's going to happen because we're both adults and because . . .

> TONY
> And because things are pretty good between us the way they are.

> ANGELA
> Right. Although things could probably be good between us the way they aren't.

> TONY
> They'd be great, Angela.

> ANGELA
> Yes, they would.

> TONY
> But they wouldn't be the same. And I don't want to take the chance of losing what we got.

> ANGELA
> Neither would I.

Although the situation serves to keep characters apart, individual character traits also contribute. Angela's sense of propriety raises questions about how far to go with Tony. Diane's intellectualism and snobbishness lead to her belief that she's above falling for Sam's lines. Maddie's fear of involvement keeps her from giving in to David.

CONTRAST IN CHARACTER RELATIONSHIPS

Contrast—more than any other quality—defines character duos. Opposites truly do attract and by contrasting two characters, the strongest character dynamics are achieved. *Lethal Weapon, 48 HRS., The Odd Couple, Shoot to Kill, Someone to Watch Over Me*—almost any relational story that comes to mind, whether a romance, a partnership, or a friendship, will probably contain contrasting characters.

Contrast can reflect behavior and attitudes. In the film *Midnight Run* by George Gallo, the behavior and approach to life of Jack the bounty hunter and Jonathan the CPA seem diametrically opposed. Their contrasting qualities include choice of jobs, relationship to their spouses, moral choices— and even eating.

> JONATHAN
> Are you familiar with the word, arterial sclerosis?
> If you want, I'll outline a complete balanced diet
> for you. Why would you eat that?

> JACK
> Why? Because it tastes good!

> JONATHAN
> But it's not good for you.

> JACK
> I'm aware of it.

JONATHAN
Why would you do something that you know is not
good for you?

JACK
'Cause I don't think about it.

JONATHAN
But that's living in denial.

JACK
I'm aware of that.

JONATHAN
So you're aware of your behavior, yet you continue
to do things that aren't good for you. That sounds
sort of foolish, don't you think so, Jack?

JACK
Stealing 15 million dollars from Jimmy Serrano
sounds foolish . . .

JONATHAN
I didn't think I'd get caught.

JACK
Now that's living in denial.

JONATHAN
I'm aware of that.

Sometimes the ethnic background, economic class, and
methods for approaching problems are contrasted. Marty Cohan and Blake Hunter describe these dynamics: " 'Who's the
Boss?' contains a number of role reversals—the blue collar and
the white collar, the working woman and the housekeeper

man as well as the contrasts of New York and Connecticut, the WASP and the Italian. Tony is very honest, straightforward, even blunt at times. He can be temperamental, and prone to bursts of anger. Tony might fly off the handle a little quicker than Angela, who tries to say 'Let's keep the peace.' Angela tends to gloss over things, bottle things up, be a little uptight in certain areas, while Tony just cuts through all the bull and gets right to the heart of the matter. Angela as the controlled businesswoman is going to try to keep her cool and not blow at the client or at the boss and Tony doesn't have this same context, he doesn't check himself like she does. Both are very family oriented and home oriented, but Angela, by her own admission, is a bit of a klutz in the kitchen, and probably struggling a little more to keep all the balls in the air with motherhood. Tony is direct, no-nonsense, he's strict with his children. Angela is more conservative, more uptight, more permissive with her children. She's more upwardly mobile, and ambitious for herself, whereas Tony is ambitious for his daughter. So there's contrast in ambition, in goals, in attitudes toward the children."

Sometimes the contrast is psychological. In "Moonlighting," the contrast between Maddie and David can be described in terms of inner fears, as well as outer characteristics. Certainly on the surface they're very different.

Carl Sautter: "She's ice, he's hot. Maddie is a bubble detached from her emotions, while David's emotions are very raw and on the surface. He's much more of a man of the moment. The thing they're most afraid of is falling in love with somebody—being exposed. But they deal with this differently. Maddie protects herself with the incredible way she looks and the coldness of her exterior. David protects himself with the fast-talking jive. So, immediately, what you've got are two characters who happen to have an enormous bond going on underneath and so you start to get that push-pull in their relationship.

"Some of their contrasts are unexpected. We did a show where they got into a discussion about God. And the obvious choice, given the focus of those characters, is that Maddie would be very prim and proper in her belief in God and David would be very irreverent about it. Glenn Caron [the creator of the show] said, 'No, let's layer them by giving them exactly the opposite attitudes.' And he switched their attitudes and made David the one who is very religious and believes in God, and Maddie the one who is very skeptical. Which worked so much better than the other—because it's not the switch you expect in it.

"You see differences in how they both react to a client. In one episode that Debra Frank and I wrote, this woman walks in and says she's a leprechaun. David instantly wants to believe her, and Maddie thinks she's nuts. They have different attitudes toward life. In this episode, Maddie says to David, 'You have no poetry in your soul. You're crass and illiterate'—and basically David's retort was, 'What you have is an artificial sense of poetry, art exhibits, and the formal side of it. Your sense of romance and poetry is an artificial one. You're the kind of person who wouldn't have clapped for Tinker Bell.' "

Here the contrast extends to the psychology that drives them. It's an understanding of their emotional lives, their fears, their vulnerabilities that opens up these characters to audiences, helping them see past the persona to something—perhaps some hurt, some tenderness—underneath.

Even in a short commercial, characters are often created through contrasts. Sometimes these contrasts are related to physicality and function. In the Bartles & Jaymes ads for wine coolers, created by Hal Riney, we see two homespun farmer-entrepreneurs, Ed and Frank. They are described through contrasts. Frank is a motor-mouth, Ed the silent sidekick. Ed is known as the true brains of the outfit. He's smarter than Frank (Ed uses the word *platitude*, which Frank admits he doesn't understand) and he's the experimental one. In one ad, "He engaged in a scientific program to determine which foods go well with wine coolers. So far, Ed has only found two foods which don't. Kohlrabi—which is a vegetable sort of like a

turnip—and candy corn."[1] Even physically they look different. Ed is tall and slim, while Frank is a stout man in sus-
penders and spectacles.

These ads, which have won a Clio Award, the ad industry's
Oscar, made Bartles & Jaymes the top-selling wine cooler, and
Frank and Ed two of the nation's most recognizable product
spokesmen.

WHERE DO YOU FIND CONFLICT?

Conflict comes from the contrasts between characters. It can
come from different ambitions, different motivations and backgrounds, different wants and goals, and attitudes and values
that are diametrically opposed to each other.

Sometimes these conflicts are psychological. The qualities
that are the most infuriating to each character are the qualities
that come from their "repressed" side (or even from their
shadow). It is the opposite quality that both attracts and repels
them.

Sometimes the conflict occurs because of a lack of directness. Misunderstandings lead to conflict. In "Cheers," even
the moment of Sam and Diane's first kiss is filled with conflict.

> SAM
> What is it you want, Diane?

> DIANE
> I want you to tell me what you want.

> SAM
> I'll tell you what I want. . . . I want to know what
> you want.

> DIANE
> Don't you see, this is the problem we've had all
> along. Neither of us is able to come out and state
> the obvious.

SAM

You're right. So, let's state the obvious.

DIANE

O.K. You go first.

SAM

Why should I go first?

DIANE

We're doing it again.

SAM

Diane, just explain one thing to me. . . . Why aren't you with Derek?

DIANE

Because I like you better.

SAM

Really? Well, I like you better than Derek, too.

DIANE

Sam . . .

SAM

All the jealousy I ever felt for my brother is nothing to what I've felt in the last five minutes.

DIANE

Oh, Sam. I think we're about to start something that might be kind of great, huh?

SAM

Yeah. Yeah. You're right. I guess we oughta like . . . kiss, huh?

And because nothing is direct with Sam and Diane, the kiss still takes another seven pages of discussion and arguing before it finally happens.

HOW DO CHARACTERS CHANGE EACH OTHER?

It's not unusual to hear an executive or producer ask, "Does the character change and grow?" Some of the strongest stories show the impact that one character can have on another.

Carl Sautter says, "The icy Maddie allows herself to be spontaneous because of the influence of David. He teaches her something about warmth, and she teaches him something about discipline. Maddie makes David less shallow, more adult. David gives Maddie a sense of humor."

In "Who's the Boss?" Angela has come off her high horse as a result of Tony's influence, and Tony has gained more confidence as a result of Angela's support. According to the show's creators, "Tony, at the beginning of this year, went to college. That would have never happened if he hadn't met Angela. I think Angela has loosened up a little. She's learned how to kick her heels up. She's learned how to relax a little, and she's a warmer person."

In a television series, if the characters were totally transformed, the dynamic of the series would be destroyed. As a result, changes are minimal. In films or novels, conflicts can be resolved and transformations can be completed by the end of the story.

Rain Man is a story about two characters who change each other. Since Raymond was so very limited emotionally, the challenge in creating the characters was to figure out how much of a transformation could realistically happen in this kind of a story. The film uses all of the elements we've mentioned in this chapter—attraction, conflict, contrast, and transforma-

[103]

tion. Barry Morrow explains: "One of the choices was making them brothers. That holds them together. And the relationship they both have to Raymond's inheritance binds them. Virtually every other way you can think of they repel one another. Age, height, intelligence, the way they walk and talk, every part of their being wants to go in opposite directions. I think attraction and repulsion are the two dynamics going on and contrast is a direct result of creating that. The transformation happens because Charlie gets worn down. . . . There was six days in the car, about two days more than he could handle, and those two days are what made him human.

"A curious thing happens across the arc of the movie. Raymond, in his own inimitable fashion, begins to wear down Charlie's ugly side—even through something as simple as language. In the beginning of the picture, Charlie is swearing a lot. But Charlie becomes civilized by being forced to care, and by the surprises he encounters. He gets rid of a lot of rough edges and becomes sensitive."

EXERCISE: Think through your relationships with friends, lovers, spouses, relatives. In what ways do your relationships fit these criteria of attraction, conflict, contrast, and transformation? Do you have a relationship with anyone in which the dynamic between the two of you is so strong that it could be the basis for the creation of a story?

CREATING CHARACTERS USING THESE ELEMENTS

You can apply these elements—attraction, conflict, contrast, and transformation—to love affairs, friendships, partnerships, any kind of character relationships.

In "Cagney and Lacey," the many contrasts between the characters added to the life of the series. Some come from the broad strokes of their characters:

Chris Cagney	*Mary Beth Lacey*
She's single, childless.	She's married, with children.
Her life revolves around her friends.	Her life revolves around her family.
She's oriented to her career.	She's oriented to her family/personal life.

Some of these contrasts come from different attitudes to the same subject:

She's for law and order.	She's more of a humanist—for individual rights.
She's Pro-Choice, but does not believe in abortion for herself.	She's Pro-Choice—and has had an abortion, and as a result defends strongly the woman's right to choose.
She's against censorship, and wouldn't censor pornography.	She's against the message of pornography, and dislikes being constantly bombarded by images that demean women.
She's against strikes.	She would never cross a picket line.

And some of the contrasts come from the differences in their temperaments and their emotions:

She finds intimacy difficult and lives alone by choice.	She's in a warm, intimate relationship with her husband.
She easily flies off the handle.	She's patient.
She's a workaholic and drinks too much.	She's balanced in her life.

[105]

Notice, through these examples of conflicts and contrast, how many story possibilities come about because the dynamic of the characters is clear and strong. Just by looking at this list you can see potential for stories about the interplay of characters as they confront the bombing of an abortion clinic, pornography, child abuse, and so on.

In starting to create a character who needs to dynamically relate to another character, one approach is to brainstorm the four elements. This is workable for any kind of story (novel, play, film, or television), but can be particularly important in a television series that depends on getting enough material from these character relationships to keep creating new stories week after week. Brainstorming can also be helpful in the creation of supporting characters, since they often interact with the lead characters.

We used this brainstorming technique when I was asked to give a seminar for the producing and writing staff of the series "MacGyver." Part of our objective for the day was to expand upon a character who had been on the show once before and seemed to have the strength and interest for the expansion of his role. The producers felt that this character would add another dimension to the character of MacGyver, particularly since the latter easily could become a character who was too much alone, too nonrelational.

The character we brainstormed was Colton—the bounty hunter. The plan was to make Colton a foil for MacGyver, as well as to develop a friendship between them over the course of a number of episodes. The actor playing Colton (Richard Lawson) joined us.

Using the same concepts discussed in this chapter, we decided to brainstorm the contrasts and conflicts between the two characters. Our list looked like this:

MacGyver	Colton
At home in the country	Out of his element in the country, at home in the city
Responsible	Carefree and unattached
Lives on a houseboat	Lives in a van (hates being on water because he's not in control; he can swim but doesn't like to)
Solitary	A loner because of lack of trust
Decides, then acts	Acts first, then decides
Indirect, nonviolent	Believes in the direct approach with the gun
Introspective	Talkative, extraverted
Cares about the means	Cares about the end
Vegetarian	Eats junk food
Environmentalist	Litterbug
Diplomatic	Blunt

As we continued to discuss the characters, it became important to understand Colton's backstory. Some of it was modeled on Richard's own experience, which was comfortable to everyone in the group. Colton had been a Marine medic in Vietnam, as had Richard. Richard described how men in war often feel closer to the medic who cares for their wounds than to anyone else, turning to him for advice, sharing fears, or just wanting to talk. When Colton left Vietnam, he decided he never wanted to be depended upon again, and chose to become insular, a loner.

We expanded on some of the ideas on our list. Colton would

not like MacGyver's houseboat. It's not on solid ground and he would feel out of control. He would have trouble with Mac-Gyver's sense of responsibility, questioning why he allows himself to get saddled with people's problems. He is particularly hostile to an ugly dog that MacGyver inherited when a friend died.

Although Mac does not particularly like the dog, he's sympathetic to it. The discussion of the dog led us to a discussion of the transformational arc of both characters. As we analyzed the effect each character has upon the other, our new list included four major entries:

1. Mac learns that sometimes it is better to follow his heart and instincts, rather than his head.
2. Colton learns patience, to wait before shooting, to sometimes think before acting.
3. Mac receives romantic advice from Colton. Some of it is good.
4. Colton learns to trust again. He learns teamwork, that sometimes there are things that can't be done without help.

As we worked with the character of Colton, our understanding of the character of MacGyver began to deepen. His attitudes, vulnerabilities, and backstory all became clearer when contrasted with those of the other man. The ideas we brainstormed certainly were only beginning steps for the further development that the writers would do together. However, we discovered that focusing on the supporting character served as an impetus for new ideas about the protagonist and the relationship between the two that could expand the show as a whole.

The stronger the dynamic between the characters, the more successful the show can be and the more possibility there is that it will remain on the air for many years.

CREATING THE TRIANGLE

Usually two characters form a relationship. Occasionally a threesome—the triangle—is the focus. Such relationships are dynamic, sometimes frightening, and usually very difficult to work out. They follow many of the concepts already discussed with the addition of certain other elements.

Fatal Attraction and *Broadcast News* both revolve around a threesome. By analyzing these films, it is possible to gain some insights into how to work with these relationships.

The relationships in both of these films are built on contrasts.

In *Fatal Attraction*, Beth and Alex are contrasting characters—one lighthearted, one depressed; one a caring wife, one a manipulative mistress; one involved with family, one single; one optimistic about her life, one desperate and pessimistic about the direction her life is taking.

In *Broadcast News*, Tom, the pretty boy who's not particularly smart, contrasts with Aaron, the smart one who's not as romantically appealing to Jane. Tom is more confident, Aaron more insecure. Tom is successful and gets what he wants, while Aaron fails miserably when he achieves his short-lived goal of being anchor.

In the triangle, the lone female or the lone male is confronted with a choice.

The drama from a triangle can come from either the difficulty of the decision or the consequences of the decision.

In *Fatal Attraction*, Act One focuses on Dan's choices. He begins by making a choice to have a one-night stand with Alex. At the end of Act One, he decides not to see her again. The consequences of his choices become the basis of Acts Two and Three.

In *Broadcast News*, Jane tries to choose between Tom and Aaron throughout the film. The story is about the difficulty of the decision. James Brooks explains: "I wanted to write a true triangle, and to me a true triangle is not loading the deck. Generally, in a triangle, there is always at least one bad guy or one flawed guy or one sexless guy—one easy choice. I determined that I would not decide which man she ended up with at the beginning of the piece—the piece itself would dictate that decision. The minute she got close to one of the men in the writing, I would bring her toward the other. I never imagined I couldn't bring her to either man, but that's how it turned out."

The writer's challenge is to explore the difficulty of the choice, and the potential attractiveness of both choices. Although in *Fatal Attraction* the choice about Alex was made early, nevertheless in Act One it was clear that she was an intelligent, attractive woman. She had more energy and seemed to be more fun than Beth, and was certainly more sexually accessible than Beth. There was, in Act One, the possibility of an ongoing relationship with Alex. Dan made the choice against this possibility. Alex made the choice to fight for the man she loved.

The choices must not be obvious, nor too one-sided, or the triangle suffers. If the choices are also moral choices, the dynamic is strengthened.

In *Broadcast News*, Jane feels her integrity is at stake if she chooses Tom, particularly after she realizes that he manipulated a news story. In *Fatal Attraction*, Dan faces moral choices throughout: when to tell his wife, how to be fair to Alex, and what his responsibilities are to both women.

The most workable triangles occur when each character exercises willfulness and intentionality.

If one character sits back, refusing to act or react, the

triangle will suffer. The triangle achieves its dynamic because there are three, rather than two, people causing twists and turns in the story.

In *Fatal Attraction,* Dan's decision sets the plot in motion. It looks as if his intention (to have a one-night affair) will be easily realized. But he has not counted on Alex. At the end of the first night, Alex decides that she wants another day with Dan. Her intention convinces Dan. After the second night, Dan's intention contradicts hers. She wants him to stay, he wants to leave. It looks, briefly, as if his intention has won. He has not counted on Alex's persistence. Her intention sets the course of events for Act Two, weaving a web that Dan tries to escape. Up to this point, the relationship emphasis has been on Dan and Alex. But Beth is a dimensional character who has her own ideas and reactions to these events. At the beginning of Act Three, when she hears about Dan's affair, her intention begins to guide the action, forcing Dan and Alex to resolve this relationship.

The film would not have worked if any one of these three characters lacked intentionality. All do their part in pushing the action.

This intentionality leads to conflict.

In each character duo, there are potentially two conflicts: the relationship from each person's point of view. With the triangle, it suddenly becomes six conflicts.

In *Fatal Attraction,* at various times in the story, Dan has a conflict with Alex and one with Beth. Beth has a conflict with Dan and one with Alex. Alex has a conflict with Dan and one with Beth. The nature of these conflicts, seen from each character's point of view, is slightly different. Alex wants to take Dan away from Beth. Beth wants to preserve her stable family life, and her own self-esteem, which won't allow her to live with a man who's betrayed her. Dan wants to preserve the status quo—something he can no longer do. Each of these conflicts is very complex, and understandable from each character's point of view. Because the writer has been able to explore the inner and outer dynamics of each character, the story has resulted in continually raised stakes with each twist and turn in the action.

Each of these conflicts reveals insecurities, character flaws, bad decision making, and desperate emotions.

None of the characters are perfect—all are driven by their own personal psychology, and by the issues unresolved in their own lives.

In *Broadcast News*, Jane has never been able to figure out what she wants. She's opinionated, obsessive in her work, too smart for her own good. Aaron has his own identity crisis, not realizing that his talent doesn't lie with being an anchor. He's sometimes petulant, insecure, even contrary. And Tom has given up the struggle about integrity, being less smart, less aware, and less concerned than Jane or Aaron. As James Brooks explains, "I worked really hard to have three flawed people, to make it true. I could tell you what was really deeply wrong with the characters, what needed fixing at the center of them. Tom is not qualified for his job. He has no sense of purpose and nothing to serve beyond himself, but he has great manners, good feelings, and decency, a sense that life should be fun and that responsibility begins and ends at home. Aaron is brilliant, dedicated, has a great sense of integrity, but has something of the intellectual snob in him. He snipes at people. Jane borders on compulsive behavior. But she has a deep feeling of purpose, she will always come through for people. She is so damn right, so damn special, that she was pulled along by her brain instead of having control over it, which is another definition of compulsive behavior. So I thought about these characters in terms of their flaws. But I also constantly try to figure out what makes somebody a hero—what are their special qualities? I think we know about weakness. I think we can all get frailty from ourselves and our imaginations, but to understand what's heroic about humanity takes some time and thinking."

Character flaws are sometimes the catalyst for the story. Certainly Dan's decision to have a discreet affair could be seen as a flaw in his character. Jane has trouble making a decision because of her own imperfections.

Both of these triangles are stronger because the characters are complex, with their own struggles, their own emotional drive, their own willfulness.

Often, character flaws and imperfections occur because at least one of the characters is driven by the shadow side of his or her personality.

Dan, in *Fatal Attraction*, is a traditional, happily married man—a nice guy. The shadow side of his personality is deceitful, secretive, lustful. It is this shadow side, not his happily married, loyal, family-man side, that is attracted to Alex. Alex, on the surface, is an attractive, high-powered, sexy, career woman. Her unconscious is driven by feelings of insecurity and desperation that cause her to misinterpret Dan's response to her.

When creating a triangle, generally one of the characters (maybe more than one character) will be driven by this shadow side. Although it isn't as evident in *Broadcast News*, it is clear in a number of stories with triangles, such as *The Phantom of the Opera* and *Dangerous Liaisons*.

In *Dangerous Liaisons* Madame de Torville is tremendously virtuous, but her shadow side (sensuality and desire) push her into a liaison with Valmont. Amazingly enough, the shadow side of Valmont is virtuous. This is rare, since the shadow side generally is thought of as the dark or negative side of a personality. But the shadow, technically, means that which is "in the dark," or the repressed side of the personality. In Valmont's case, he has an innate decency. It's his ability to feel and give love that has been repressed and that gets awakened by Madame de Torville. The conscious side of his personality is deceitful, manipulative; the unconscious side contains love and empathy and caring.

The triangle is strengthened if something is hidden from the other characters.

Motives may be hidden: Beth doesn't know that Alex is actively seeking to take her husband away from her. Actions may be hidden: Jane doesn't know that Tom faked the news story. Attitudes may be hidden: Beth doesn't know about Dan's attraction to Alex. Jane doesn't know that Aaron is in love with her.

Sometimes what is hidden is some quality of the character's psychology that drives the story and character, yet isn't even known to the person. Alex is probably unconscious of the power of her desperation. She's unconscious of her projection on to Dan, of her misinterpretation of the relationship. Her unconsciousness further complicates the story.

These hidden qualities—whether inner or outer—have the potential to drive the characters to a crisis. An important moment in this kind of story is the *reveal*—the moment when what has been hidden is found out. When Beth finds out about Alex, her actions create a crisis in her marriage. When Jane finds out about Tom's dishonesty, the discovery leads to a crisis in her developing relationship with him.

Working out character triangles is analogous to juggling many objects and keeping them constantly in play. Some of the knottiest script problems I've encountered have involved the creation of the character triangle. There is much for the writer to sort out and to figure out. However, in spite of the complexity, some of the most powerful character relationships have come from this complex relationship.

A CASE STUDY: "CHEERS"

"Cheers" is an example of a series that has had to go through a number of new discussions of character dynamics, since there have been several changes in the show during its long history. It premiered in the fall of 1982. In the 1984–1985 season, one of its major actors, Nicholas Colasanto, who played the role of Coach, died. The creators of the show had to decide what kind of a character was best to replace him, a character that would keep the same dynamics. In 1987, Shelley Long, who had played Diane, left the show. The creators had to decide how to replace her, to create a new character dynamic for the show.

James Burrows, one of the creators (along with Glen and Les Charles) and a director of many episodes, explains the process:

"We wanted to do a show about a sports bar, and we wanted to create a Tracy-Hepburn relationship. We liked the contrast of that relationship: Miss Uptown, Mr. Downtown. The pragmatist, the idealist. The guy that says it can't be done and a woman that says it can be done. It's a clash everybody knows. It makes for great marriages. So the original idea of the show was that a girl owned the bar and a guy worked for her. But when the script was written, the writers came up with the idea of a college student who wanders into a bar that is run by the ex-jock.

"As we further defined the characters, we made Sam an ex-alcoholic, and we gave Diane a father who died and a cat who died in the first year. We gave new dynamics to their characters by getting them together and taking them apart.

"So in creating these characters the challenge was in keeping Diane upper-crust and sympathetic and to keep Sam a jock but not to make him too dumb.

"We decided also that we wanted to do an evolving sitcom, where the characters change throughout the series. Not all the

[115]

critics liked this, since most sitcoms don't evolve; but we liked it and found it gave our characters more definition—more that we could explore.

"So those were the things we tried to do, and they wrote a script, and it was wonderful, and we were lucky enough to get two actors to play it who had incredible chemistry. That's what it is. It's luck, casting. Those two people came in and made those characters come alive so that the characters became more important than the bar.

"We tried to create strong relationships with the supporting characters also. We always felt that Carla had the hots for Sam, which she did and still does, and we always felt that she was at odds with Diane because Sam liked Diane. She would pick on Diane and you'd feel sorry for Carla, so she would get away with being hostile. Now those dynamics over the years evolved and they were great. I think that subliminally Carla felt Diane was smarter than she was. She might have been smarter on an intellectual level, but Carla's street smart. Diane's home life was happy, Carla's wasn't. Carla's saddled with a number of children, Diane is free.

"The sitcom is driven by the character conflict. In the early days, it was the chemistry between Sam and Diane that drove it—and how Carla reacted to Sam, everybody reacting to Cliff and how much of a loudmouth he is. With these kinds of characters, we could do a simple show like Diane borrowing some money from Sam and then before paying him back buying sweaters and clothes for herself, and his reaction of, Why can't she pay me back?

"With Shelley leaving the show, now, we're back to the old original premise, which is about a woman who owns the bar. Everybody loves Sam. So that's the entrée to the show. If we were to lose him we couldn't do the show. It's Sam's bar and he's the one people feel comfortable with. With the arrival of Kirstie [who plays Rebecca], we've gone back to everybody being important—it's more of an ensemble show now.

"When we first created Rebecca, we thought of a character

who was a total bitch. We had decided not to go comedienne, since I don't think you can find anybody funnier than Shelley. We decided not to go blonde, not to go with another waitress. Kirstie was the first actress we saw. Jeff Greenberg, our casting director, came in and said, 'I've got the lady for you.' So Kirstie read for us, and she had this vulnerable quality, and none of us had ever seen or thought of this in that role. I remember Teddy saying after the reading that he wanted to hold her. And we thought about it and we said this would be a different way to go, but it may be a great way.

"Kirstie added neurotic, a scatterbrain, to our character description. And it worked. The show has new life.

"When we saw this direction for Rebecca, we started to create her backstory. We found out she went to the University of Connecticut and had a nickname, and was a failure in other jobs.

"With this new character, there was a new set of dynamics to create between Rebecca and Sam. We thought it would be funny that she was a woman that was not attracted to Sam and he couldn't believe it. And, of course, he had to react to her like he reacts to any girl: 'I can have her anytime I want her.' We haven't progressed with that as much as we had with Sam and Diane—their characters haven't moved that much in these two years—although they have become friends.

"Rebecca also changed the dynamics with other characters. Rebecca and Norm have a great relationship. They care for one another. We felt in one show that Rebecca needed to talk about herself. If you use Sam for that function he's always going to want to go to bed with her. So we thought it would be interesting to hear Norm talk to her. He has no ulterior motive. He's a listener. This way we could get out more information about her life.

"Carla's suffered a little because Rebecca was her boss and she couldn't take shots at her. So their relationship isn't as dynamic as Carla and Diane. But we did give Carla a husband. So she could play off that.

"We also had to replace Nick Colasanto since he died during the end of the third year. We knew for a year he was sick. We had some time to figure out what to do. We had to have a bartender. We had no choice. We didn't want to go old, we wanted to go young. 'Family Ties' was getting such a big youth audience ahead of us, so we had to go young to get the youth in. We had to go dense, because Nick was doing the dumb jokes. On a comedy it always helps to have somebody who's not too together because you can do dumb jokes and explain the plot to them. It's a good writing device. So we decided to go farmboy. Woody wasn't the conception. The conception was a thin kid with big teeth and Woody came in kind of like a hokey farmboy, and he was hysterical. There was no question he was the best.

"Woody and Coach are both quite similar—they're both doing the same kind of joke. You do lose the 'father figure,' which Nick had. With Woody you have more like a son. But you lose little else.

"We've gone through a number of overhauls and changes in the show. It's rather a miracle that these changes have worked!"

APPLICATION

The concepts I've discussed can work with any kind of relationships. Whether between main characters or supporting characters, creating a stronger relational dynamic can bring life and excitement to your story. As you think of your own characters, ask yourself:

- Is there conflict between my characters? Is it expressed through action, through attitudes, through values?
- Have I contrasted my characters so there are differences between them?
- Do my characters have the potential to transform each other? Will the audience or reader understand why

these two people should be together? Is the attraction between them clear? Is the impact they have upon each other also clear?

SUMMARY

Drama is essentially relational. It is rarely about people alone, but usually about people who interact with others, influence others, and who are changed as a result of this interaction.

Without dynamic relationships, characters can become bland and uninteresting. It is the conflicts and contrasts that provide drama between characters, and prove that relationships can be just as compelling and memorable as any individual character.

6

~~~

Adding Supporting and Minor Characters

Adding supporting characters to a story expands its palette. Like a painter who keeps adding details to round out the painting, a writer adds supporting characters to give further depth, color, and texture to the story.

Many of the same principles apply for supporting characters as for major characters. The characters need to be consistent, to possess attitudes and values and emotions, and often to be paradoxes.

But there are important differences. Imagine a painting of a wedding. There is much detail around the two main figures of the bride and groom. And there are many figures, most of them somewhat indistinguishable from each other. But among them there are several who are sharply and broadly drawn: a young girl in red, for instance, in the foreground, playing with a kitten who has wandered into the scene; the minister, looking self-important, in full view as he stands on the top steps of the church; the mother of the bride, in a bright yellow lace dress, hovering near her daughter, weeping with joy.

In this picture, the supporting characters are just as memorable as the major ones. Although there are some who are indistinguishable (the guests who are the extras), there are others who round out the story being told, and who expand upon the theme of love and marriage.

In many cases, supporting characters have taken over the story, becoming more important than the writer originally intended them to be. Sometimes this improves the story. In television, the supporting character sometimes becomes the audience's favorite, as in "Happy Days" and "Family Ties," when the Fonz and Alex came to the forefront.

James Burrows says, "If you've got a good subsidiary character, you use him till the cows come home. You don't shy away from him. Diane's boyfriend Frasier was originally just a device we brought in the third year to get Diane back into the bar. But he became wonderful, we continued to use him."

Dale Wasserman agrees. "Sometimes supporting characters are more interesting than major characters because the major characters have the burden of moving the story forward. But the supporting characters don't have that burden, and consequently can be more colorful."

Sometimes this takeover can be dangerous. The story can become unbalanced if the supporting characters don't know their place. To better understand what that place is, let's look at a process for creating supporting characters. This process includes:

- Deciding what the function of the character needs to be
- Creating a character that contrasts with other characters to fulfill that function
- Filling out that character by adding details

THE FUNCTION

To begin, ask yourself: Who is necessary, besides my protagonist, for the telling of this story? Who does my major character need around him or her?

By clarifying these issues, you will prevent yourself from arbitrarily adding characters to the story, and will begin to understand who is needed and who is not. The objective is to find the balance between the main characters and the supporting characters, and not to confuse the story by overloading it with people.

A supporting character can serve several functions in a story. These include helping to define the protagonist's role, conveying the theme of the story, and helping to move the story forward.

The supporting character helps define the role and importance of the protagonist.

If characters are defined by their role or their job (e.g., mother, corporation president, cashier at the restaurant), you will need to create characters surrounding them that help clarify that role.

Mothers need children around them to show that they really are mothers. Corporation presidents have vice presidents, secretaries, chauffeurs, and bodyguards. Restaurant cashiers are surrounded by waiters, managers, cooks, busboys, and patrons. How many of these characters you use, and how much you emphasize them, will depend on the needs of the story. But your protagonist's position will not be clear without some of them.

When "Midnight Caller" was created, it was clear to the writers that Jack Killian would need characters surrounding him in order to do his work. Richard DiLello, creator of the series, explains: "We created three supporting characters. He had to have an engineer—some operator taking calls—and that became Billy Po. Clearly there had to be some mole into the police department to help on the stories that are crime oriented. What could be more natural than his former commanding officer, Lieutenant Zymak? Devon is the producer, the rescuing angel that came along. She had to be someone that was bright and attractive and intelligent, someone that was as strong as he was."

Notice in this scene how both Devon, the producer, and Po, the engineer, fulfill their functions and support the main character.

Killian is reviewing his copy. He looks up at Billy Po in the control room. Billy boots up the computer. Jack takes his copy and throws it into the wastebasket.

> DEVON
>
> What are you doing?

> KILLIAN
>
> I can't read this crap.

> DEVON
>
> What do you mean you can't read it?

> KILLIAN
>
> Let me wing it. . . .

> DEVON
>
> No. I'm sorry. I wrote this for you—

> KILLIAN
>
> Do you really think we have time to argue about this now?

Killian nods at the ON THE AIR sign as it comes to life. Devon takes a deep, resigned breath and leans into the microphone.

> DEVON
>
> It's the Midnight Hour and this is Devon King on KJCM Radio, 98.3 on your FM dial. . . . Tonight, on KJCM, we're pleased to announce the birth of the Midnight Caller. A program that puts you in the driver's seat. . . . Jack Killian recently re-

entered civilian life. He'll be taking your calls and
answering questions about police work and pro-
cedures. . . . However, it should be noted that
Jack Killian's opinions are not endorsed by the San
Francisco Police Department. . . .

DEVON	PO
. . . nor do they necessarily reflect the opinions and poli- cies of the management of KJCM.	KJCM. Midnight Caller. Thanks for calling. What's your first name and where are you calling from?

DEVON
And so, without further ado, we're pleased to
introduce you to Jack Killian—

KILLIAN
The Nighthawk!

Devon throws Jack a look but continues without missing a beat.

DEVON
Our host on Midnight Caller.

(Later) . . . The ON THE AIR light goes off. Devon turns to
Jack.

DEVON
The Nighthawk?

KILLIAN
Yeah. You like that?

DEVON
Not particularly.

Supporting characters help convey the theme of the story.

Most writers have something important and meaningful they want to communicate through their story and characters. The supporting characters are an opportunity to express the theme, without the story becoming talky or pedantic.

To do this, the writer needs first to think through the theme. It might be about identity, integrity, community, tyranny, fame, love, or some other idea. Once the theme is set, each character can begin to express it.

Ordinary People is a story about the search for identity and meaning. Judith Guest explains, "Just as Conrad and Calvin are able to be transformed because of the challenges of the tragedy in their life, there are other characters who continue to live a shallow existence. They represent the 'unexamined life.' So every character, to some extent, stands for the two sides of this theme. The psychiatrist Burger, Calvin, Conrad, Jeanine, and Carole all expand the idea of the 'examined life'—the people who live life on a deeper level. Stillman, Ray, and Beth show the people who live life superficially, and who are unwilling (or unable) to be transformed."

One Flew Over the Cuckoo's Nest explores the theme of the relationship of the rebel to authority. Related themes convey repression, tyranny, and empowerment.

The supporting characters of this play convey the fear, the desire for safety, the repression, and the yearning to be strong. Here are three statements by three different supporting characters that expand these themes.

Dr. Spivey is part of the repressive rules, but also a pawn to the tyranny of Nurse Ratched.

DR. SPIVEY: Ther-a-peutic Com-munity. That means that this ward is Society in miniature, and since Society decides who is sane and who isn't, you must measure up. Our goal here is a completely democratic ward, governed by the patients—working to restore you to the Outside. The important thing is to let nothing fester inside you. Talk. Discuss. Confess. If you hear another patient say something of significance, write it down in the Log Book for all to see. Do you know what this procedure is called?

MCMURPHY: Squealing.

The patient Harding recognizes his weakness, but is powerless to do anything about it.

HARDING: The world belongs to the strong, my friend. The rabbit recognizes the strength of the wolf, so he digs holes and hides when the wolf is about. He doesn't challenge the wolf to combat. Mr. McMurphy . . . my friend . . . I'm not a chicken, I'm a rabbit. All of us here, rabbits, hippity-hopping through our Walt Disney world! Billy, hop around for Mr. McMurphy here. Cheswick, show him how furry you are. Ah, they're bashful. Isn't that sweet?

The Columbia River Indian, Chief Bromden, sees the repression clearly, but doesn't feel "big enough" to fight it.

CHIEF BROMDEN: I can't help you, Billy. None of us can. As soon as a man goes to help somebody, he leaves himself wide open. That's what McMurphy can't understand—us wanting to be safe. That's why nobody complains about the fog. As bad as it is, you can slip back into it and feel safe. [1]

Each of these characters exemplifies a different part of the theme of repression. Dr. Spivey is the spokesman for authority, who takes part in the limiting of other people's responses by always being ready to report them. Harding and Bromden represent the unwillingness to fight it, and the desire to be safe.

Supporting characters can be catalyst figures, giving out information that moves the story forward.

Samuel, in *Witness*, provides John Book with the information he needs to do his job.

> BOOK
> I'm a police officer. Samuel, I want you to tell me everything you saw when you went in there.

> SAMUEL
> I saw him.

> BOOK
> Who'd you see?

> SAMUEL
> The man who killed him.

> BOOK
> Okay, Sam. Can you tell me what he looked like?

> SAMUEL
> He was like him.
> (Samuel points to Carter, John's partner.)

> BOOK
> He was a black man. With black skin?

> SAMUEL
> But not schtumpig.

> BOOK
> Not what?

[127]

RACHEL
On the farm, a pig born small in the litter is schtumpig. A runt.

SUPPORTING CHARACTERS ADD
COLOR AND TEXTURE

The kind of character you create to fulfill a function in a story is not an arbitrary decision. Once you know who you need, the next step is deciding what colors and textures will round out the design of your story. There are a number of different choices you can make.

Contrasting your characters will give you the strongest strokes.
This may mean contrasting a supporting character with the protagonist, or contrasting supporting characters with each other. Contrasts between different characters may be physical contrasts, such as light and dark, heavy and slim, fast and slow. They may be contrasts in attitudes, such as cynical and optimistic, innocent and sophisticated, hostile and happy-go-lucky, passionate and cold.

Contrasting characters are particularly important in ensemble shows. Bill Finkel, writer-producer from "L.A. Law," talks of the many contrasts that are built into the characters in that show. Although some of them might be considered main characters rather than supporting characters, Bill says, he wouldn't know how to make a meaningful distinction. Thus their inclusion here.

"There are contrasts in their attitudes toward their work. Brackman is managerial, he is primarily focused on the financial well-being of the firm, whereas Kuzak is somebody who has more of an ideological bent. He's interested in a more active, moral, political agenda. Becker is intensely materialistic, more of an egoist, more interested in self-aggrandizement than everybody else in the firm. Markowitz has a certain melding of a bottom-line mentality owing to being an accountant and a tax lawyer. Kelsey is socially conscious, with feminist instincts.

"There are contrasts between ethnicity and class. Victor Sisifuentes is a Hispanic from East L.A. He's conflicted by his relative success in the Anglo downtown L.A. legal field. He's a single guy, and handsome. He's socially conscious and basically a progressive-thinking guy. Markowitz is upper-middle-class Jewish, older and married and in the process of beginning a family at the age of forty-something. He's also an exacting, somewhat controlling guy, detail-oriented, almost smothering in his ability to kind of take over a situation and compulsively lay out the choices and alternatives.

"McKenzie is a senior partner, probably in his sixties, at the stage of his life where different things assume importance. He also has power in the firm because of being a senior partner.

"Jonathan Rollins is black and middle-class, which says something about his differentiation from blacks who might have grown up in Compton. Roxanne, the secretary, is desperate for some sort of security and a significant relationship. She's also somebody who makes much less money than the lawyers do, so she's in a different material situation and class than the lawyers she relates to.

"There is also the single-married contrast. Rollins and Sisifuentes are single; Kelsey and Markowitz are married; Abby and Brackman are divorced. Abby is a single mother, Kelsey and Markowitz are in the process of starting a family.

"There are contrasts of values, such as social consciousness versus materialism. Kuzak works in the criminal justice system. He and Sisifuentes might represent a guilty rapist, whereas Becker, who's a matrimonial lawyer, wouldn't be the least bit interested in representing someone like that.

"And there are contrasts in their style. This might include what they wear (Becker is very stylish), what kind of cars they drive (Grace Van Owen drives a vintage BMW), what kind of houses they live in, what kind of furnishings they have in their homes or offices. Sisifuentes has Diego Rivera posters in his office. Becker has cold, modern, dramatic-looking furniture. Kelsey has a southwestern-comfortable rather informal-looking office."

Minor characters can also be revealed through contrasts.

In the film *War Games,* by Lawrence Lasker and Walter Parkes, there are two minor characters who give information to David, the main character, about how to break into the computer. They could have been dull and bland. Instead, small details in contrast and rhythms are added to create an interesting scene.

Malvin is described as a "thin, hyper, postadolescent" and Jim is described as "overweight, sloppily dressed with a hint of arrogance in his expression." Malvin's nervousness contrasts with Jim's deliberateness.

> DAVID
> I want you to look at something.

> MALVIN
> What is this? . . . Where did you get this?

> DAVID
> I was trying to break into Protovision . . . I wanted
> to get the programs for their new games.

Jim reaches for the printout.

> MALVIN
> Wait . . . I'm not through.

Jim snatches it anyway. He scans it, looking askew through his thick smudgy glasses.

> JIM
> Global thermonuclear war . . . This didn't come
> from Protovision.

MALVIN

I know it didn't. . . . Ask him where he got it.

DAVID

I told you.

MALVIN

It must be military. Definitely military. Probably classified.

DAVID

If it's military, why would they have games like blackjack and checkers?

JIM

Maybe because they're games that teach basic strategy.

Jennifer quizzically watches this odd group.

MALVIN

Who's that?

DAVID

She's with me.

MALVIN

Why is she standing over there . . . she's standing right near the tape drive . . . don't let her touch it. I'm having a lot of trouble with that unit.

JIM

If you really want to get in, find out everything you can about the guy who designed the system. . . .

DAVID

Come on. How do I even find out who the guy is?

[131]

Jim ponders the problem. Impatiently, Malvin breaks in.

> MALVIN
> You guys are so dumb. I don't believe it. I betcha I
> know how to do it, I figured it out.

> DAVID
> Oh yeah, Malvin. How would you do it?

> MALVIN
> First game on the list, dummies. I'd go in through
> Falken's Maze.

Although the scene is short, and Malvin and Jim will not appear again, notice how clearly they are differentiated. The scene itself is a simple story scene. It's designed to give a piece of information that enables the story to continue. But the characters provide the interest and make an on-the-nose scene compelling and involving.

EXERCISE: Think of how you might contrast two lawyers, two policemen, two trapeze artists, two carpenters, two fraternal twins.

Occasionally characters are meant to be similar.

Instead of using contrasting colors and textures, the characters work within the same hue. For example, in *Gone With the Wind*, Scarlett's suitors are undifferentiated, so that Rhett Butler can contrast with them.

Villains and bodyguards are often similar, as are dancers in the chorus line, sailors, or office workers—whenever the characters are background and backdrop figures, and you choose not to call attention to them.

[132]

Sometimes one characteristic within a character is broadened, even exaggerated, to the extent that it totally defines the character.

This is particularly true for comic characters. Wendy, Archie's wife, in *A Fish Called Wanda*, is introduced as someone who is always experiencing some great frustration. Everything goes wrong for her: she gets a flat tire, her daughter Portia has a zit, there are cracks in her dishware, problems with a bridge game, there's no ice for her drink—life for Wendy doesn't run smoothly. Her life is always in some sort of a muddle.

An exaggerated characteristic might be physical. In *Platoon*, Barnes (Tom Berenger) is defined physically by his scar, which denotes a wealth of negative experiences. The makeup of his character connotes hardness, vengefulness, and a distortion or corruption of his soul.

Sometimes supporting characters are defined by the contrasts and paradoxes within their own personalities.

This can add a memorable touch that will give extra dimension to the character.

In the James Bond film *The Living Daylights*, the villain, a big man played by Joe Don Baker, loved the little-boy activity of playing with toy soldiers. This detail took him out of the usual villain character type.

In the Police Academy films there's the police captain who loves his goldfish. In *Airplane*, there's the middle-class woman who knows how to talk jive and the nun who's not afraid to knock some sense into a panicked woman.

Such touches, though broad, add both humor and dimensionality to characters who may take focus for only a few moments.

There is a danger, however, in creating these character shticks. We've all seen characters with a limp, or a facial tic, or a scar—details that were created in an attempt to add interest but do nothing to dimensionalize the character or help round out the story. Rather than adding new information, they become confusing and limiting and result in a caricature.

Character shticks work best when they pay off in the story, and when there is a compelling reason for them to exist. In *A Fish Called Wanda*, Otto reads Nietzsche to prove that he's not dumb. In *Airplane*, the jeopardy of the situation caused confusion and panic. The jive-talking woman and the punching nun functioned by solving the problem.

Occasionally, the color or background of the character creates a character type.

Character types are not meant to be stereotypes. They aren't defined by their role, gender, or ethnic background (as in the "dumb secretary" or the "cool black") but are defined by their action. They are meant to be so broadly drawn that they are instantly recognizable to audiences.

Throughout the history of fiction writing, writers have relied on types. In Roman plays, types included the braggadocio soldier, the pedantic scholar, the parasite, the foolish father, the shrew, the fop, the tricky slave, the scheming valet, the buffoon, the trickster, the rustic. In later plays, we have seen the scheming maid, the lovestruck lad, the fool. And melodrama took the type as far as it could go, giving us such cardboard figures as the villain twirling his mustache, the handsome hero, and the sweet young thing.

In the above cases, the defining characteristic—foolish or pedantic, etc.—never says that "all fathers are fools" or "all scholars are pedantic," but that within the larger classification of fathers or scholars, there's a certain type that's a fool or a pedant. Whereas a character type can be an important element in many stories, a stereotype only limits the story. (Stereotyping will be discussed in more detail in Chapter 9.)

Sometimes it is important to use a type. "When you're creating minor characters for a TV series," says James Burrows, "you try to make them on the nose. If you've got a bully, you try to cast a bully. If you cast a guy who's a bully, but doesn't look like one, it will take the audience too much time to figure out that character. Whereas if you cast a bully everybody can identify, you can then work on working him off the other characters, and making him funny."

Character types can be broadly drawn, or they can be drawn with great attention to detail. Tartuffe (from Molière's play) is a character type, a hypochondriac; Polonius from *Hamlet* is a doddering father; but both contain considerable detailing.

When the acting teacher and director, Constantin Stanislavski, worked with actors, he encouraged them to continually add great detail to their portrayals. His description of the process can be of help to writers creating a character type.

"It is possible to portray on the stage a character in general terms—such as a soldier. For instance, a professional soldier as a general rule holds himself stiffly erect, marches around instead of walking like a normal person, clicks his heels together to make his spurs ring, speaks in a loud, barking tone out of habit. . . . But this is oversimplified . . . and passes for a portrait but not the character. . . . These characters are traditional, lifeless, hackneyed portrayals . . . not live people but figures in a ritual. Other actors, who possess more acute powers of observation, are able to choose subdivisions in the general categories of stock figures. They can make distinctions among military men, between a member of an ordinary and a guard's regiment, between infantry and cavalry, they know soldiers, officers, generals. . . . Other actors add a still more heightened, detailed sense of observation. We now have a soldier with a name, Ivan Ivanovich Ivanov, and with features not duplicated in any other soldier."[2]

Although it is not the job of the writer to put the pauses, the gestures, the exchanged looks into the script (this is the work of the actor), there still needs to be some sharp definition of the essence of the character that goes beyond broad generalities.

Actors cannot act generalities—and a general character will not attract an actor to the role, or a reader to the book.

FILLING IN THE CHARACTER

By understanding the function, and adding color and texture, you will come close to creating a fully realized character. But it may also be necessary to add details that come from your own observation, and through your own experience.

Sometimes this means putting yourself into the character. Seth Werner, creator of the California Raisins commercial, comments, "A lot of people have said that the people that I put into commercials have a little bit of me in them. Somebody said you could pick me out in the line of dancing raisins. It's the way I walk and the way I would dance. The commercial is a little off the norm. And that's what gives it a little personality and magic. Even when our animators were actually making the raisins out of clay, you would see them look in a mirror and make an expression and copy it on the face of the raisin. I think work should come from your heart, and when it does, other people feel it. It reaches. It's hard to say what it is exactly, but it is these small touches and subtleties that make it special."

Robert Benton created a number of his characters for *Places in the Heart* by remembering and observing people he had known. "I had a great-uncle who was blind. I was sitting with my relatives talking about the script when one of them reminded me of my Uncle Bud. We started telling stories about him and he became the basis of Mr. Will. With Will I wanted to show a man who is very smart, who had lost his eyesight, who had cut himself off from life and through the course of the movie is reintroduced back to his life. I wanted a kind of intelligence and kind of an anger about his life. Now my uncle had the intelligence, but not the anger. I wanted to get a sense that Will was out of keeping with the rest of the people, that he was a little more sophisticated, a little more neurotic than anyone else. Will gives contrast and a varied texture to the story. Everybody in that town can't be nice small-town people. Somebody has to be different from that.

"Margaret and Vi are based on an amalgam of two or three people I had known. They were based on people I had gone to high school with.

"I particularly loved the character of Wayne. I grew up in the Southwest in the thirties and forties with hillbilly music, and hillbilly music was about grand passion. I wanted someone with a grand passion and a set of problems that weren't what you'd think of as being in a small, God-fearing town. Country-western music was about 'Don't rob another man's castle,' and about going out honky-tonkying, and it was about great passions in this most ordinary setting."

Supporting characters, like major characters, are created through small details. Even if they are less important characters, they still can be sharply drawn.

CREATING THE VILLAIN

There is one other character that must be discussed, who is sometimes a major character, sometimes a supporting character. That's the villain.

Everything mentioned up to this point will be useful for creating the villain. But the villain presents some unusual problems.

By definition, the villain is the evil character who opposes the protagonist. Villains are usually the antagonists, although not all antagonists are villains. Antagonists won't be villains, for example, if they oppose the protagonist not out of bad motives but because it's their function in the story. If the main character wants to go to Harvard but doesn't have the grades to get in, the representatives of the school will become the antagonists since they are opposing the protagonist, but they won't be villains. The role of the villain always connotes evil.

Whether villains wear black hats (as in the old Westerns), or fly fast jets and commit corporate crime, they place problems in the path of the "good guy," and generally wreak social and personal havoc.

On the simplest level, stories that contain villains are usually stories about good and evil. Usually the protagonist stands for the good, and the villain opposes the good. Most villains are action-oriented. They steal, kill, betray, wound, and work against the good. Many of them begin to look alike. Often there's a tendency for them to be poorly motivated, and one-dimensional. The reasons for their evil actions are rarely explained, as if people do evil just because they feel like doing it.

It is possible, though, to create dimensional villains. Depending on the style of the story, and how much depth you want to bring into it, villains can be just as unforgettable as any other character. Certainly such characters as Captain Bligh in *Mutiny on the Bounty*, Salieri in *Amadeus*, or the particularly dimensional villains in the miniseries "Holocaust" come to mind as well-drawn villains.

To understand the villain, it's helpful to understand the relationship between the good and evil that exists in most stories.

F. Scott Peck, in his book *People of the Lie*, defines evil as live spelled backward, i.e., as that which opposes life. Using this definition, the good character stands for an affirmation of life. He or she stands for saving the ranch for the sake of the family (*Shane* and *Places in the Heart*), for overcoming abuse (*Nobody's Child*, *The Burning Bed*), for self-esteem (*The Color Purple*), for realizing one's potential (*The Karate Kid*, *Heart Like a Wheel*), for reaching out to others (*Rain Man*), for recognizing the humanity of those unlike ourselves (*Bill*, *E.T.*), for the promotion of growth and transformation (*The Turning Point*).

Evil then opposes good. It tyrannizes, restricts, represses, puts down, defies, and puts limits on others. Whether he employs obvious evil, such as murder and other forms of violence, or some of the more subtle forms of abuse, the villain has the same function in the story: to work against the good.

What are the different approaches to creating dimensional villains? First of all, it is necessary to ask why they act the way they do. Their motives can be explained through exploring the villain as victim, or the villain as self-serving agent. In the first case the villain is defined through reaction; in the second case, through action.

For many villains, the doing of evil comes as a result of negative influences in their own lives. As a writer creating this kind of a character, you might explore the backstory, looking at social and personal factors that might have created these negative characteristics. You would recognize that nobody is "purely bad," and round out the character by showing good points, complex psychology, and emotions such as fear, frustration, anger, rage, and/or envy. Most analyses of real-life violent crimes focus on the "villain as victim," searching out the reasons, perhaps, why a quiet, unassuming man murders someone. Emphasis is usually placed on a difficult and unstable family life, often poverty and abuse, repression of the person's feelings, and a solitary, nonrelational life-style.

If you choose to create an active, rather than a reactive, villain, you could dimensionalize the character through exploring the complex unconscious factors that motivate him or her. It has been said "No one is a villain in his own eyes." No one believes he is doing evil. Most villains justify their actions, thinking they are doing it for a greater good. These people usually have strong defense mechanisms. They're unaware of the unconscious forces driving them. Generally they are driven by their shadow side, and are continually justifying their actions.

Don Corleone in *The Godfather* is partially motivated by love of his family. Although Gordon Gekko in *Wall Street* admits to being motivated by greed, to him, "greed" is a good word, connoting accomplishment and success and ambition.

If you were creating villains, you would try to discover the greater good, or what they consider the greater good, that is driving them. Is it a desire for safety? Love of family? Security (for themselves or others close to them)? A better world (perhaps a world of one class and one color)? Although such a motivation might have positive aspects to it, it will take form in negative actions because of a desire to impose the villain's value system on others. Ultimately, it will result in some kind of repression.

Villains may be unaware of what they do. Rather than justifying their actions, their evil actions are the result of unconscious forces that they don't understand. The violence and repression that come from these characters tend to be more subtle, but they are still effective. These villains deny their actions and their motivations, a form of denial that can be found in compulsive behaviors, addictions, and abuse. These are the characters who say, "It was only a spanking; it didn't hurt my child," or "I only had a couple of drinks, not enough to get me drunk and violent," or "I love my wife, certainly she's not afraid of me!" The villains in *The Burning Bed* and *Nobody's Child* are unaware of the negative effects of their actions.

Villains of any type suffer from a kind of narcissism, an inability to see, and respect, others' reality. It's an inability to recognize the humanity of other people, or to affirm their right to be who they are.

EXERCISE: Have you ever felt oppressed? What did your oppressor do to make you feel that way? Were covert or overt methods used? Imagine the response your persecutor might give to justify his or her actions. Could you create a villain in a story using this person as a model?

A CASE STUDY:
ONE FLEW OVER THE CUCKOO'S NEST

One Flew Over the Cuckoo's Nest began as a novel by Ken Kesey, was developed as a play by Dale Wasserman, and then became a film in 1975, with writing credit going to Bo Gold-man and Lawrence Hauben.

When Dale Wasserman wrote the play, he had to re-create the supporting characters. The characters are memorable for their broad strokes, their thematic function, and their relationship to the main character, McMurphy.

Dale Wasserman sees each character as working off of the theme. "Ken Kesey's novel deals with the philosophy of the meaning of the rebel in society. It is the prototypical idea of the rebel against authority and what happens to him. Curiously, *Man of La Mancha* [also written by Wasserman] and *One Flew Over the Cuckoo's Nest*, which seems so terribly dissimilar, are regarded as almost the same play because each of them deals with a rebel, an outcast of society, a man who won't conform. And in both cases, society is dedicated to the suppression or extermination of that man.

"The argument which I made in the play was about the standardization of society and the suppression of individuality. The whole argument is that we live in a society which must repress and discipline the individual for its own protection. It is protecting itself from the aberrations of the individuals. It's protecting its power, and unruly people threaten power.

"To make this point, I had to show the relationship between the suppression and the victims of the suppression. So all the supporting characters are victims in some way. It was necessary to differentiate each character very sharply, because victims en masse as in a concentration camp are really not very interesting. They might represent something, but they won't be well-drawn characters. I realized that it was very important that they not be a uniformed troop of some kind; so I went to great trouble to individualize them as sharply as possible.

"Each of the victims is a victim in a slightly different way. The Indian is a victim because Indians in the United States are victims. The man with homosexual tendencies [Harding] is a victim because society laughs at and scorns such people, so he voluntarily withdrew from society. The stuttering boy was a victim of a monster mother. The man who sits around making bombs all day is a victim of the U.S. Army, which destroyed his ability to function in society. The man who seems crucified on the wall is a victim of medical society, which experiments with people by performing lobotomies to bring people into a mode of acceptable behavior. And even Nurse Ratched is a victim of a standardized and disciplinarian society that has made her into a monster."

To begin filling out the characters, Dale spent ten days in a mental institution.

"One of the elements I was looking for was the level of intelligence and education of these people, and their level of articulation. I wanted to look at the particular patterns of behavior that get these people designated as insane. There's a big variation in that. In some, you see almost nothing that would distinguish them from normalcy. But because they take drugs every day, their behavior is modified, held down.

"By watching them before they were medicated and after, I could see a whole range of behavior. After taking drugs, there is very little color in their speech. It's what you call utility speech. Before drugs it reveals itself in very wild, sometimes fascinating patterns. They have a mad logic of their own. And sometimes I was very impressed by the beauty of articulation of these people. It was not conventional, coherent, or grammatical."

Dale creates interest by working against the logic of the characters.

"Perfect logic in the way characters speak and act is dull. It's generally a lie. So I look for the illogical, the inconsistent, the out of place in a character, because those things are more revelatory than the straight line of the character. For instance, if there's somebody of a brutal nature, I also watch them very carefully because they will reveal completely inconsistent attributes; and sometimes the inconsistent attributes are the ones that truly reveal the character.

"McMurphy, who seems to be a rough and brutal man, teaches inmates to dance and does it with delicacy. He also, surprisingly, quotes poetry. He sometimes misquotes it, but somewhere inside of him he had a love of it. When I look at characters, I look at them with the supposition that perfect logic is dull."

Dale also analyzes the hidden aspects of the character: "I look for underlying drive and then find ways to let the audience see things that the character doesn't know about himself. This is true of people who seem to be acting from a professed set of motives and actually are acting out of another set of impulses entirely.

"Billy Bibbit doesn't understand what his mother has done to him. He protects his mother, who is really the destructive influence in his life. Harding blames himself for what is really not a matter of his own blame—his sexual nature. Nurse Ratched is really a powerfully and artificially repressed woman who is a perfect army model. The repression has caused her to become a man hater. Curiously, she has warmth and decency. These are the interesting contradictions. She does what she does for very good reasons, which does not alter the fact that what she does is very bad.

"There's an element that I love to emphasize and that is surprise. Principal characters rarely do that, but supporting characters often do that and it wakes up an audience and keeps them alert. In *Cuckoo's Nest*, Candy Starr was the surprise. Who expects a good-looking hooker in this milieu? Even when she brings her friend, that's a surprise. Not just one hooker, but two. And then also, they are really fun girls."

I asked Dale what the problems are that can come up with supporting characters.

"One of the worst problems is lack of fulfillment. There is time to fulfill your principal characters in a story but often auxiliary and very interesting characters are left dangling and unfulfilled. And I believe that whether the audience knows it or not, it is very frustrating. I have seen instances where I desperately wished to know about what happened to auxiliary characters and there wasn't time.

"There is also a tendency to sketch in only enough characteristics that serve the character and leave the character otherwise not quite fleshed out. In movies that's almost a necessity because you don't want too much attention to go to contributory characters. It troubles me when it happens, though, because ideally every character should be interesting and shouldn't leave one baffled and dissatisfied."

APPLICATION

As you look at the supporting characters in your script, ask yourself:

- Do my characters all have a function in the story? What is their function?
- What is the theme of my story? In what way do each of my characters help expand this theme?
- Have I paid attention to the creation of my minor characters? If I use character types, have I made sure that they are not stereotypes?
- Do I have contrasting characters? In what ways do they add color and texture?
- What broad strokes have I used to define both my supporting and minor characters? Do these strokes relate to the story or theme, so they don't seem like imposed character schticks?
- Do I have villains in my story? What are their backstories? The unconscious forces that drive them? Is there a perceived good that they pursue, using evil actions to achieve it?

SUMMARY

Many of the best stories are memorable because of their supporting characters. They can move the story, clarify the role of the main character, add color and texture, deepen the theme, and expand the palette, adding detail to even the smallest scene, the smallest moment.

James Dearden sums it up: "Within the context of reality, without overdoing it, you can make your little characters interesting. A lot of what stories are about is entertainment, not in a broad sense, but in a sense of keeping people's eyes moving and their ears flapping and their brains working. It's those little details that make something come alive."

7

≋

Writing Dialogue

Many writers and writing teachers have said to me, "You can't teach dialogue. Writers either have an ear for it or they don't." I agree that great dialogue, like great painting and great music, cannot be taught. However, *good* dialogue can be. There are methods of thinking through a scene and a character that can improve dialogue. Writers can train their ears to hear rhythms and speech patterns just as musicians can train themselves to hear melodies and musical rhythms.

You first need to understand what is good dialogue—and what is bad dialogue.

- Good dialogue is like a piece of music. It has a beat, a rhythm, a melody.
- Good dialogue tends to be short, and spare. Generally no character will speak for more than two or three lines.
- Good dialogue is like a tennis match. The ball moves back and forth between players and represents a constant exchange of power that can be sexual, physical, political, or social.

- Good dialogue conveys conflict, attitudes, and intentions. Rather than telling about the character, it reveals character.
- Good dialogue is easily spoken, because of its rhythms. It makes great actors of us all.

There are a number of great dialogue writers. One of these is James Brooks. Read the following dialogues from *Broadcast News*. Then read them aloud, and listen to their rhythms. Notice that each line reveals something about the character. Notice, too, the difference between the dialogue of one character and that of another.

The assistant says to Jane:

ASSISTANT
In every way but socially, you're my role model.

Or, in a conversation between Jane and Tom:

JANE
I saw the taped outtakes of the interview with the girl. I know you "acted" your reaction after the interview. Working up tears for a news piece cutaway. You totally crossed the line between . . .

TOM
It's hard not to cross it; they keep moving the little sucker, don't they?

Or, in a conversation between Aaron and Jane:

AARON
Could you at least pretend that this is an awkward situation for you—me showing up while you're getting ready for a date.

[147]

> JANE
>
> It's not a date. It's coworkers going to a profes-
> sional enclave.

Jane, unnoticed, reaches into the paper bag, takes a small box
of condoms, and drops it into her evening bag.

Notice the elements contained in these examples. The dialogue of the assistant contains an attitude (toward Jane). Tom's
dialogue shows both emotion (frustration) and a conflict of
values as he strives for integrity in a career where the meaning
of integrity keeps changing. Aaron's dialogue shows conflict
and attitude. And Jane's dialogue shows inner conflict as she
tries to balance her relationships with Tom and Aaron.

From the above examples, we can see that great dialogue
has conflict, emotions, and attitudes. It also has another essential component: the subtext.

WHAT IS SUBTEXT?

Subtext is what the character is really saying beneath and
between the lines. Often characters don't understand themselves. They're often not direct and don't say what they mean.
We might say that the subtext is all the underlying drives and
meanings that are not apparent to the character, but that are
apparent to the audience or reader.

One of the most delightful examples of subtext comes from
the film *Annie Hall*, written by Woody Allen. When Alvie and
Annie first meet, they look each other over. Their dialogue is
an intellectual discussion about photography, but their subtext
is written in subtitles on the screen. In their subtext, she
wonders if she's smart enough for him, he wonders if he's
shallow; she wonders if he's a shmuck like the other men she's
dated, he wonders what she looks like naked.

In *Annie Hall*, both Annie and Alvie understand the subtext
of their conversation. Usually, however, the characters are

unconscious of the subtext. They're not aware of what they're really saying, of what they really mean.

In Robert Anderson's play *I Never Sang for My Father*, there is a strong subtextual scene in the first act. It takes place in a restaurant and seems to be about a son taking his father out to dinner. The subtext of the scene is quite different. It's about the lack of communication and tension between father and son, and suppressed anger from a son who doesn't live up to his father's expectations.

Although the subtext will always be partly dependent upon an actor's interpretation, I have inserted what might be the subtext of various lines of dialogue. The scene in the play occurs between the father (Tom), the mother (Margaret), and the son (Gene), but for the purposes of this discussion, I have condensed the scene and focused on the Tom-Gene relationship.

Waitress comes up for drink orders:

WAITRESS: Dry martini?

TOM: (a roguish twinkle) You twist my arm. Six to one.

(*SUBTEXT: I'm quite a man to drink my martinis this dry!*)

What's your pleasure, Gene . . . Dubonnet?

(*SUBTEXT: To Tom, Gene is certainly not as much a man as he. Therefore, he wouldn't drink martinis; he'd drink Dubonnet.*)

GENE: I'll have a martini too, please.

TOM: But not six to one.

GENE: Yes, the same!

(*SUBTEXT: I defy you to think I'm any less than you are!*)

TOM: Well!

(*SUBTEXT: What an upstart!*)

Now, this is my dinner, understand?

GENE: No, I invited you.

TOM: Uh-uh, you had all the expenses of coming to get us.

(*SUBTEXT: Look what a generous father I am—and how fair-minded! And remember, you don't make enough money to pay for this trip—and pay for my dinner!*)

GENE: No, it's mine. And order what you want. Don't go reading down the prices first. . . . Whenever I take you out to dinner, you always read down the prices first.

(*SUBTEXT: Let me give to you. I want you to enjoy the meal and yes, I can afford it.*)

TOM: I do not. But I think it's ridiculous to pay, look, $3.75 for curried shrimp.

GENE: You like shrimp. Take the shrimp.

TOM: If you'll let me pay for it.

GENE: No! Now, come on.

(*SUBTEXT: For God's sake, let me treat you to this shrimp, please!*)

TOM: Look, I appreciate it, Gene, but on what you make . . .

(*SUBTEXT: You aren't as successful as I am or as I'd like you to be.*)

GENE: I can afford it. Now let's not argue.

As the anger builds before they even have a chance to order, Tom declares: "I don't feel like anything. I have no appetite."

WHAT IS BAD DIALOGUE?

The elements that make up good dialogue include conflict, attitudes, emotions, and subtext. What, then, is bad dialogue?

- Bad dialogue is wooden, stilted, difficult to speak.
- With bad dialogue, all characters sound alike, and none of them sounds like a real person.
- Bad dialogue tells the subtext. Rather than revealing character, it spells out every thought and feeling.
- Bad dialogue simplifies people, instead of revealing their complexity.

So how do you improve dialogue if you know it's flat, bland, uninteresting, or wooden?

Let's begin with a scene that you see in many scripts. A screenwriter has been called into a meeting with a producer, who's interested in producing his script. What follows is meant to be some of the worst dialogue ever written (I take full credit for it—it was written especially for this book).

PRODUCER
Well, come in. It is a real pleasure to meet you. You know, I liked your script very much—it is really very good.

YOUNG WRITER
Well, thank you. It is my first script, and I'm really very scared about what you'll think about it. I'm from Kansas, and I have never been to a big city

[151]

before, and I feel really lucky to meet someone like you. I have admired your work for so many years.

PRODUCER
Oh, that is very nice of you to say that. Let's talk about making a deal.

Pretty dreadful, isn't it? It's wooden. It's boring—no life or energy to it. Both characters tell us just what they're thinking and feeling. Both characters sound the same.

To begin with, this dialogue can be improved about 5 percent by doing nothing else but writing contractions instead of "it is" or "I have," and by taking out all such excess words as "well," "oh," "you know." Simply making it more conversational will begin to improve it. But to make the dialogue work, the scene needs to be rethought.

I asked for help from one of my clients, a writer named Dara Marks, whose dialogue always has energy and rhythm. We worked through the process in much the same way I would work through a consulting session on dialogue. I asked the questions; we discussed; she rewrote.

We began by looking at different aspects of the scene. First we asked, *Who are these people?* We know the writer is from Kansas, he's new to Los Angeles and admires the producer. We know nothing about the character of the producer.

What are producers like? The producer stereotype is a frenetic dealmaker who's out to make a lot of money, or a fifty-year-old, cigar-smoking shark, hungry to exploit young talent. Dara and I agreed that, while any stereotype has some truth in it, most producers are quite different from that. We discussed producers we had met: those who were very relaxed and laid-back (or high), those who played tennis every afternoon, those who were nervous, those who were self-important, those who were very knowledgeable about all aspects of film.

We discussed the various *settings* where we've met

producers—in their offices, in restaurants, in a hotel suite if they're from out of town, in a home office, at a party, or on a racquetball court. Since we've both actually had meetings on a boat, that's where we decided to set our scene. We created a producer in his early fifties, very successful, who runs his business from the main salon off the large, airy aft deck of his ninety-foot yacht.

Picking a more unusual setting (but one that is entirely believable in Hollywood) gave us opportunities to move away from the traditional and the predictable—and to create more interesting and real characters.

We then thought about the *attitudes* of our two characters, and decided that the producer would be asleep at the top of the scene, and the young writer would be overly excited and eager.

Keeping these three elements in mind, we reworked the scene in the following way:

INT. YACHT—DAY

TIGHT ON a pencil that rolls back and forth across the top of a desk as the yacht sways softly in its anchored berth. The CAMERA WIDENS to first reveal the soles of two deck shoes perched cross-legged on the desk, then the entire slumbering form of the PRODUCER comes into FOCUS. Like a baby in a crib, he rocks gently from side to side with a half-finished script laid out across his chest.

The YOUNG WRITER appears at the cabin door, slightly off balance, and very uncomfortable at being on a boat (this is probably his first time off dry land). Awkwardly, he looks around and sees that the producer is asleep. He doesn't quite know how to handle this.

                    YOUNG WRITER
     Ah-hem.

The PRODUCER doesn't move.

[153]

> YOUNG WRITER
> (louder)
Ah-hem . . .

The PRODUCER casually opens one eye and glances at his watch.

> PRODUCER
You're late.

> YOUNG WRITER
I'm sorry, sir, but the bus . . .

> PRODUCER
> (sitting up)
You rode a bus? . . .

> YOUNG WRITER
> (very uneasy)
Well, yes, sir . . .

> PRODUCER
I never knew anybody who rode a bus.
> (He jots down a note to himself.)
Gotta try that.

The PRODUCER lights up a cigar, which only serves to make the YOUNG WRITER more seasick.

> PRODUCER
So, kid, what can I do for you?

> YOUNG WRITER
> (surprised)
It's my script, sir, you asked to see me.

[154]

> PRODUCER

I did?

YOUNG WRITER nods.

> PRODUCER

What's it called?

> YOUNG WRITER

"They All Came Running," sir.

The PRODUCER rummages through his desk.

> PRODUCER

Let's see, running . . . funning . . .

The YOUNG WRITER sees his script and points it out to the PRODUCER.

> YOUNG WRITER

That's it.

> PRODUCER

Oh, yeah, the running script . . .
Running's out this year, hockey's big.

> YOUNG WRITER

It's not really about running, Mr. Dinklemyer. It's about Kansas, where I'm from.

> PRODUCER

Kansas, huh? Sorta corny and homespun?
> (thinks for a beat)
Could start a new trend—I like it! Okay, kid, you gotta deal!

In this reworking of the dialogue, notice that the producer's attitude is leading the scene. He has an attitude about new experiences (he might try taking the bus sometime), about Kansas (it's homespun and corny), and an attitude about commercial trends (he's successful because he has a "nose" for what's hot and what's not).

The dialogue now has some rhythm, an unusual setting that could be used by actor and director, a feeling for the producer's character, and an attitude for him. But we still don't have much of a sense of the young writer.

To begin developing his character, we began with his backstory. We decided that he has come out to Los Angeles and has given himself exactly a year to sell his script. This is the last day of the year, and at this point, he figures he has nothing to lose. He is angry, frustrated, and feeling a bit hopeless about the whole situation.

Just as the producer leads the scene through his attitude, we decided that the young writer will lead the scene through conflict and emotion.

We then reapproached the scene, keeping most of the elements we liked from the last draft, but now focusing on the young writer's contribution to the scene:

INT. YACHT—DAY

The YOUNG WRITER sticks his head inside the door, and is very annoyed to see the PRODUCER sound asleep.

> YOUNG WRITER
> Ah-hem.

The PRODUCER doesn't move.

> YOUNG WRITER
> (very loud)
> Ah-hem . . .

The PRODUCER awakes with a start, embarrassed to be caught napping.

> PRODUCER
> (fumbling to pull himself together)
> You're late!

> YOUNG WRITER
> (amazed)
> I've been here since nine this morning.

> PRODUCER
> Well, I'm a busy man.
> (shuffles some papers around his desk)
> So, what'd'ya got?

> YOUNG WRITER
> About six hours before I gotta be on a bus back t'Wichita.

> PRODUCER
> You ride the bus?

> YOUNG WRITER
> Something wrong with that?

> PRODUCER
> No, I just never knew anybody who did that before.

> YOUNG WRITER
> Well, we're the people who watch your movies. You oughta try it sometime.

> PRODUCER
> I don't think I like your attitude.

YOUNG WRITER
(blowing his cool)
I'm not selling my attitude, sir! I'm selling my
script, so either buy it or I'm going back to the
farm.

PRODUCER
What farm? What script?

YOUNG WRITER
(exasperated)
The script you wanted to see me about.

PRODUCER
I did? What's it called?

YOUNG WRITER
"They All Came Running."

The PRODUCER rummages through his desk.

PRODUCER
Running stories went out with disco!

YOUNG WRITER
It's not really about running, for God's sake, it's
about the plight of the displaced dirt farmer in
Kansas.

PRODUCER
Dirt, huh? Who cares about dirt?

YOUNG WRITER
(throws his hands up in the air)
I give up! I'm going home. . . .

[158]

PRODUCER

Wait a minute!
    (thinking aloud)
Dirt, earth . . . Homespun, I like it. Could start a
new trend. O.K. . . . You got a deal. . . .

The YOUNG WRITER is startled. He stops in his tracks and
spins around.

YOUNG WRITER

    (excited)
You mean it?

PRODUCER

Sure, kid . . . But we gotta change the title!

Now we have two equal characters, each contributing to the
scene through attitude, conflict, backstory, and intention.
With stronger characters, the dialogue has become stronger.

If you were to continue working on this scene, there are
several different directions you could take.

You might decide that the scene has too much of an "edge"
to it, that both characters are a bit too angry and adversarial.
You might decide to give the edge to one character, but not to
the other. Perhaps the writer is angry, but the producer refuses
to get hooked by his anger.

You might decide to add "business" to this scene, detailing
the individual activity of each character. Think for a moment
about some of the more unusual meetings you've had. What
has gone on in those meetings, besides simply talking?

I was once in a meeting where the executive had about fifty
Mickey Mouse figures all over his desk. If you used this, you
might have the producer dusting them throughout the meeting.

I've been in meetings where an executive played darts most
of the time. Or where the producer spent most of the time on
the phone, while sizing me up across the desk.

Perhaps there's something going on in the other room that adds to the business of the scene. Dara and I considered giving the producer a wife who is creating a large sculpture out on the deck using all sorts of machinery. Throughout the scene, the writer would be trying to identify sounds that remind him of machine guns, or drills, or a motor with a problem. This could lead to an attitude of fear or curiosity or simply an inability to concentrate on anything the producer is saying.

Any of these suggestions for business could be used to reveal character, and to communicate subtext so the scene is not on-the-nose.

You might decide to explore the atmosphere of the scene to create other directions for the dialogue to go. Is the room cold or hot? Is it dark or light? Is someone smoking? Is there a strange smell in the room? How is the room furnished? Are there books and scripts on every chair, so there's no place to sit?

You might think about changing the race, gender, age, or weight of one of your characters. Any of these changes can also change the dialogue. I once had an appointment with a person (not a producer) who weighed about 400 pounds. He sat in a very large chair—and never moved. My surprise at his appearance made the first few moments very uncomfortable—and everything said at the beginning of the meeting was simply a babble.

The expectations that one has of a meeting will affect the dialogue. If your character expected to see a producer who is fifty, and the producer is actually twenty-five, the unexpected situation can change the dialogue. If one of the characters is wearing an eye patch, or a neck brace, or has an eye tic, or is trying to hide a very small pimple on his chin—all of this can affect the dialogue.

The language or vocabulary used will also change the dialogue. If a character has an accent, or uses very big words that the other character doesn't understand, or uses "in" vocabulary that is not clear—the type of communication between characters will change.

The context of the scene can also have an impact on what is said during the scene. Perhaps the producer is going through a divorce, or the young writer has just come from a funeral of a close friend. These situations will affect the direction of the scene. Some other contexts might be: the scene is the beginning of a love affair, or the end of a long working relationship between producer and writer, or the producer had just hired another writer but felt he had to keep the appointment anyway.

The producer and young writer scene has been written many times before. One of its most unusual settings occurs in Moss Hart's autobiography, *Act One*. This book has been adapted for a feature film by one of my clients, Treva Silverman ("The Mary Tyler Moore Show") and is to be produced by Laurence Mark (*Working Girl*) and Scott Rudin (*Mrs. Soffel*).

The scene takes place in New York. Moss Hart, a new writer, has just finished his play, and has received word that the great theatrical producer, Jed Harris, wants to meet with him about his script. Notice how simple much of the dialogue seems—yet when combined with business and attitude, how much it communicates about these two men.

INT. MADISON HOTEL—DAY

It's 12 o'clock and Moss, eager and excited, is at the concierge desk.

MOSS
Moss Hart to see Jed Harris.

CONCIERGE
Go right up. Suite 1201. Mr. Harris is expecting you.

MOSS
(grins)
Thank you.

CUT TO:

INT. MADISON HOTEL, 12TH FLOOR—DAY

Moss gets out of the elevator, walks down the hall in great spirits. He gets to suite 1201, knocks softly at the door. It's halfway open. No answer. He knocks again, then presses bell.

VOICE
(muted; in the distance)
Come in, come in.

CUT TO:

INT. SUITE 1201—DAY

Moss hesitantly walks into the suite. He passes through a little foyer into the living room. It is immaculately clean, looks almost unlived in. Not a cigarette butt or newspaper around. Is this the right place?

MOSS
(calls softly)
Excuse me . . . Moss Hart for Jed Harris.

VOICE
Yes. Come in.

He follows the voice, hesitantly. He crosses from the living room to the bedroom.

CUT TO:

INT. BEDROOM—DAY

One twin bed is slept in, the covers kicked off. The other bed is piled high with scripts. Two ashtrays are filled to the brim with half-smoked cigarettes. The shade is drawn, the room is in half

darkness. Moss is totally confused, frightened he's made some
mistake.

> MOSS
>
> Hello?

> VOICE
> (from bathroom)
> Come in. Come in.

He approaches the bathroom and takes a few steps forward.
Moss's expression: terrified, horrified, stunned.

> CUT TO:

We see JED HARRIS from the back, standing by the sink,
shaving. He is naked.

> JED HARRIS
> (casually)
> Good morning. I'm really sorry I couldn't see you
> till now.

> MOSS
> (totally nonplussed; shakily)
> That's . . . all right.

Moss looks around, trying to find where to focus.

> JED HARRIS
> Actually, I wanted to read your script earlier, but
> you know the way this season is going. . . .

> MOSS
> (addressing his shoe)
> Oh, yes. Oh, yes.

JED HARRIS
Last night there was that party for the Lunts. . . .
Everybody seems to adore the Lunts. As far as I'm
concerned, one Lunt is enough.

Moss laughs, a dry, raspy gasp that stops as soon as it starts. Jed
Harris starts to towel-dry his face.

JED HARRIS
But I went to the party because there was this
little Italian actress. There'd been a lot of intrigu-
ing gossip about her that I wanted to check up on.

A towel drops on the floor from the sink. Moss stares at it, not
sure whether he should pick it up. He finally decides not to.
Jed Harris, continuing his conversation, winks at Moss. Moss
tries to remember what Jed Harris is talking about.

JED HARRIS
The gossip turned out to be truer than I'd even
hoped.

He laughs smugly at Moss. Moss tries a smile, but can't get it to
happen. He succeeds in more of a facial tic.

The scene, in many ways, is quite simple. Notice, however,
how many levels are conveyed through the dialogue and the
business of the scene. Moss's attitude includes anticipation,
shock, embarrassment. There are hints of conflict over
whether to enter or not, whether to pick up the towel or not,
whether to speak or not.

Jed conveys a nonchalance and delight over his evening's
escapade with the Italian actress. Treva created this conversation because, as she said, "Moss Hart wrote his memoir in the

1950s, in a more innocent time. I needed to dispel any hints that Jed Harris appearing nude could be any sort of a homosexual overture."

The scene in Moss Hart's book includes the same setting and circumstances—Jed Harris's nudity and Moss's embarrassment, but the focus is different. Hart recounts,

> There is no question in my mind but that Jed Harris is one of the finest conversationalists on the subject of the theatre. . . . Even in my disoriented state, I could tell that this was theatre talk of a kind I had never heard before, and as the haze of my embarrassment began to lift with each succeeding article of clothing that he put on, I began to listen intently. His criticism of *Once in a Lifetime* was sharp, penetrating, full of a quick apprehension of its potentialities as well as its pitfalls, and included an astonishingly profound understanding of satirical writing in general. His nimble tongue raced from *Once in a Lifetime* to Chekhov, to a production of *Uncle Vanya* that he was contemplating, to a scathing denunciation of his fellow producers, to a swift categorizing of certain American playwrights whose plays were not worth the paper they were written on, and back again to *Once in a Lifetime*—in a dazzling cascade of eagle-winged and mercurial words that left me a little breathless. [1]

Converting this paragraph into dialogue for a script could easily have yielded a very talky scene. Treva says, "In order to begin to re-create this, I would need to include obscure, esoteric information that would be a total turnoff to audiences."

I was the consultant on the project, and we decided to cut the scene since the film is really about Moss's relationship with George Kaufman, not with Jed Harris. However, the scene is a personal favorite of mine because of its clarity of emotions and quiet charm.

TECHNIQUES FOR
APPROACHING DIALOGUE

Many writers love the sounds and rhythms and color of good dialogue.

Playwright Robert Anderson says, "I fell in love with dialogue when my brother brought home a Noël Coward play in college. I picked it up and asked my mother what it was and she said it was a play. From then on I was fascinated. I've always been drawn to dialogue in novels. When reading novels, I would skip to the dialogue, which is a mistake, because in novels the story's not carried in the dialogue, it's in the narrative.

"I don't think you should even start to be a playwright if you don't have a feel for dialogue. I think a playwright should have a gift for dramatic situation and for dramatic dialogue."

Writers prepare themselves for writing dialogue in a number of different ways. The first step for most of them is to spend a tremendous amount of time working out the story, before any dialogue is ever written.

Robert Anderson continues, "I give a lot of thought to the dynamics of a story, the structure, the characters, what they're doing, the subtext, what's going on in each scene, the progression of each scene. I will spend months working on what this play's going to be about. I call it fishing. I sit at the desk every morning and throw my idea into the pond and I make notes and I never look at those notes again. And the next day I throw the same fish hook in and see what comes up. And after a while something begins to take shape and form. Then I see where the characters are, where they're going, what it's about, and then I put it all away, and write the first draft of the play in about two or three weeks. Red-hot heat, never reading a word till the draft is finished. So it's a combination of spontaneity within a shape.

[166]

"I lay out the structure of the scene, six or seven months or however long I've been working on the notes. I know the characters pretty well. They can talk about anything they want as long as it accomplishes the purpose of the scene. Writing dialogue reminds me of a conversation I had with my friend, the playwright Sidney Kingsley. I knew that Sidney was writing a play so I asked him how he was doing. He said, 'I'm almost finished, I'll start writing the dialogue tomorrow.' So the dialogue comes after everything else has been mapped out."

Dale Wasserman approaches dialogue by first analyzing the subject and intention of each scene: "Dialogue comes last with me. When I know where my story is going and when I know what the arguments and the intent of each scene are going to be, then I add the dialogue. By that time the dialogue and its content has become almost inevitable. Of course, the color and style of dialogue is not inevitable and one sweats over that a great deal. To give it the kind of simplicity and style that it needs can be very difficult."

Many writers train their ear by listening carefully to people's speech in a variety of situations:

John Millington Synge said that by listening to the scullery maids talk, he got his sense of the dialogue.

Robin Cook says he loves to overhear people talk on airplanes, and he plays basketball in the park and listens to the kids teasing each other.

Robert Benton will sometimes record dialogue to hear a rhythm. "In *Places in the Heart*, the character of Margaret Sparling was based on a friend of mine. I sat with her and I tape-recorded her for two days. We simply talked and talked until I had her language down."

But real talk isn't the same as dialogue. So developing an ear for listening to dialogue is only one step. The next step is translating real talk into fictional dialogue.

"I never use words that people actually speak," says Robert Anderson. "If you set up a tape recorder where people are talking and play it back, it's ridiculous. All dialogue is stylized, verisimilitude and not reality. One has an ear for bridging that gap. Many years ago, when I was writing for a radio show called 'The Theatre Guild on the Air,' I did an adaptation of A Farewell to Arms to star Humphrey Bogart. To my dismay, I found I could use very little of the famous Hemingway dialogue because it didn't carry the story forward or develop the character relationships. When the show was broadcast the critics said, 'The Hemingway dialogue carries the show.' I was flattered that I had been able to write Hemingwayesque dialogue . . . which carried the story forward."

Robin Cook says, "Whenever I write any dialogue I read it aloud. I'm looking for similitude. I want it to sound like two people talking together. It's so obvious to me when I read a book in which the dialogue isn't realistic. One of the amazing parts of really good dialogue is that it gives you the impression of being in the vernacular without being in the vernacular."

According to Shelley Lowenkopf, "Dialogue in a novel was never intended to be an exact representation of speech; it represents the attitude of the characters. You should be able to tell who is speaking by what he or she wants. So dialogue should be an outpouring of the secret part of the character. Part of constructing good dialogue is to think through and understand what a character wants to keep secret."

Leonard Tourney adds: "Realistic dialogue is not real talk, it is an artifice. Dialogue should characterize, be very compressed. It gives the flavor of reality."

There are exercises and processes that writers can do to help them write good dialogue.

Treva Silverman begins by talking into a tape recorder and then listens to it the next day. "By that time I've forgotten 90 percent of what I've said, and I can listen to it as if I'm hearing it for the first time. The thing that I'm looking for at that point is some sort of hint of what the character sounds like. Once I get the voice, I can relax, but it's hell until that happens. It's much easier with the tape recorder, less intimidating. I'm not staring at a blank sheet of paper, I'm not staring at an empty screen."

Robert Anderson says, "Many writers start writing dialogue first, rather than last. Neil Simon once told me he works that way. They say they discover the characters and the story line of the play as they go along. After trying this a number of times as a young man (after all, I loved dialogue, not story) I found I came a cropper too many times after forty pages. Dead end. I had discovered nothing. In writing the dialogue I can discover things I didn't know about myself, things I didn't know I knew, but I can't seem to discover story. I have to know my ending.

"If you have the wrong situation the dialogue won't flow. Unless you have people in an interesting situation, interesting in terms of progression of the scene, it's deadly.

"The playwright John Van Druten said sometimes he couldn't get a character to speak properly until he changed the name. I've sometimes said that. I've said a Laura will speak differently from a Hazel, and until you get the right name—it won't work.

"I used to give my students dialogue exercises. With one exercise, I said somebody had found a ten-dollar bill in the street and he argues at the kitchen table over how that ten dollars is going to be spent. The movement of the scene is who's going to spend the ten dollars and how, but the entire subtext can illuminate the tensions in the whole family.

"In my play *You Know I Can't Hear You When the Water's Running*, there's a scene where two middle-aged people discuss whether they're going to buy twin beds or keep the old double bed. Ostensibly they're arguing about the beds but the entire marriage is revealed in that argument. The subtext is about what has happened to their life and their love and middle age."

When Jules Feiffer taught a playwriting class at the Yale drama school, he helped students improve dialogue by "getting rid of self-indulgence and other conceits, deciding what the point of the scene is, and cutting out everything but the point. Cutting out those flourishes that particularly young writers like to put in to prove how brilliant they are."

The key to writing good dialogue begins with learning to listen for rhythms and nuances.

"The most important thing," Robert Anderson says, "is to develop a voice. It's not just in dialogue, but in attitude. If you have a voice, the dialogue is going to come out right."

A CASE STUDY: JULES FEIFFER

Many of us are familiar with Jules Feiffer's work through his weekly cartoons. His film (and later the play) of *Carnal Knowledge* has often been discussed in terms of its brilliant dialogue. He also adapted *Popeye* for the film, wrote *Little Murders* and *Elliott Loves*. His comments about dialogue are relevant to all fiction forms, with many of those on cartoon characters particularly relevant to the advertising field.

In this interview, he talks about the difference of writing dialogue for each medium.

"When I moved from cartoons to theatre and later to film I learned that the dialogue in each is very, very different. In theatre and in film, when you're dealing with relationships, you have to show the beginning, the middle, and the end stages, and not just the end, which is what I do in the comics. What people say to each other in cartoon form is very elliptical and very short. It has to be because of the circumstances of space. Particularly on the stage, you can afford more nuance, a lot more indirectness. Stage dialogue can be fuller and more expository—and more ego gratifying—than film dialogue. On film you can afford a lot more nonverbal communication—eye exchanges, physical movement, etc."

I asked Jules about the process by which he creates dialogue.

"First of all, I don't think in terms of dialogue. Dialogue is something that comes naturally after you get the character and after you put the character in the situation. Once you put two or more people together in some sort of situation, and have already decided who and what they are, they're going to automatically say certain kinds of things. One thing will lead to the other and you're going to discover along with your audience what it is they're talking about. I've often been surprised at what my characters have had to say to each other. You get them going and they take off on their own, which is when it really becomes fun. I find that if I follow an outline, I'm not going to get anything very interesting and very lively, and a lot of what characters have to say to each other provides the energy for the piece. Energy is what's important in terms of relationships. Even if the situation is essentially a passive one, there's got to be some real presence of energy.

"This energy comes from the subtext. This is the underlying conflict which is at war with the surface of the piece, so the only real conflict may be between this character and himself or herself. Working with subtext is not a matter of working it out with notes on it. It's a matter of understanding perfectly what's really going on, what's not going on and why it's not, and how much of it will show on the surface. And the struggle of the piece is how to disguise it until very late in the day when all sorts of things will start topping out and will create the dramatic climaxes.

"At some point the subtext will rise to the surface, but if it rises totally to the surface I don't think you're doing yourself a service. Some part of it has to rise, but you can't give away all your secrets. You have to leave some of those for the audience to work out for itself. I want the audience to be another character in the movie, to be actively involved. If you cross every *t* and dot every *i*, and treat the audience like a couch potato, then there is no energy that goes between what happens onstage or on film and the audience sitting there registering. I know that I as a member of an audience always love to be forced to think and be challenged by the work I'm presented with and I like to do the same in my work.

[171]

"If the cartoon is personal rather than political, it will often deal with subtext. If it's political, it may be more to the point; but, even then, since it's almost always ironical, it will have to do with subtext. At least in my work, most of the people who talk are in the business of not relating. People often, whether in their public lives or private lives, will say the opposite of what they mean or disguise their meaning in all sorts of labels. That's been the focus of my work since the very beginning. To strip those labels and show what the point really is.

"If I had trouble getting into a scene, I often found it helpful to begin with dialogue such as, 'Hello, how are you. I'm fine. What are you doing today? Not much. Well, I have this problem . . . ,' and going on for pages of meaningless blabbering until I got into the scene. Other times I've entered the scene from the very middle, then backed up. At times I've been stuck for days and even weeks. One play took me six years because I couldn't get the hang of where I was going.

"If you can grasp the sense of that thought process and put it into the ordinary language you speak, you've gone a long way. Then in the next draft, revise it with different conversational or speech flourishes to denote certain characters. In too many plays and too many screenplays, everybody sounds alike. I like my characters to be so individual that their names aren't necessarily on the page for the reader—they know who's speaking. You have to train yourself to hear behavioral tics in conversation, but more than that you have to hear your own inner voice."

APPLICATION

Dialogue is key to writing for the theatre, but it is essential to any kind of fiction writing, whether drama, novel, or short story.

As you look at your own characters, ask yourself:

- Have I defined character through speech rhythms, vocabulary, accent (if necessary), and even length of sentences?
- Is there conflict within the dialogue? Does the dialogue contrast attitudes of the various characters?
- Does my dialogue contain subtext? Have I addressed what my characters are really saying, versus what they do say?
- Can I tell from the dialogue the cultural or ethnic background of the character? The educational level? The age of the character?
- If I didn't see the names of the characters above their dialogue, would I be able to tell that different characters were talking? Does the dialogue differentiate the character?

SUMMARY

A writer is always in training. Learning to write dialogue includes listening, reading, and speaking good dialogue to internalize the sounds and rhythms. Some scriptwriters take acting classes to further understand what the actor needs from them.

Dialogue is the music of fiction writing, the rhythms and melodies. It is possible for any writer to develop an ear for it—and to write dialogue that conveys attitude and emotions, and that expresses the many intricacies and complexities of character.

8

Creating Nonrealistic Characters

So far, we've been discussing realistic characters—characters who are like us. We identify with them because they share our same flaws, our same desires and goals. They are not superheroes, nor do they have subhuman characteristics or exaggerated faults.

But the world of fiction is also filled with nonrealistic characters. Think about the broad range of characters who come from a special world of the imagination—E.T., Mr. Ed, mermaids and swamp things and killer tomatoes, Superman and Batman, King Kong, Bambi and Dumbo, the Jolly Green Giant, and the California Raisins.

In this chapter, we will look at four different types of nonrealistic characters that you, as a writer, might create. They are the symbolic character, the nonhuman character, the fantasy character, and the mythic character. The characters within each category are determined by their limits, by their context, and by the associations and responses that the audience brings to each.

THE SYMBOLIC CHARACTER

Realistic characters are the most dimensional, defined by consistency and paradoxes, by complex psychology, attitudes, values, and emotions. If you were to write down the number of qualities possessed by a dimensional character, you would end up with a very long list.

Symbolic characters are one-dimensional. They are not meant to be dimensional. They personify one quality, usually based on an idea such as love, wisdom, mercy, or justice. They work best in nonrealistic stories, in myths, fantasies, or even within an exaggerated comic-book style such as the superhero stories.

The roots of the symbolic character are found in Greek and Roman tragedies. The gods and goddesses were generally defined by one attribute. Athena/Minerva was the goddess of wisdom, Aphrodite/Venus the goddess of love, Hades/Pluto the god of the underworld, Poseidon/Neptune the god of the sea, Dionysus/Bacchus the god of wine, Artemis/Diana the goddess of wild things.

Although limited in their dimensionality, they are not necessarily bland or uninteresting, since the one quality implies a number of related qualities.

For instance, Mars (or Ares) was the god of war. Detested by his parents, Zeus and Hera, he is ruthless, murderous, and bloodstained. He's accompanied by Discord and Strife, and by Terror and Trembling and Panic. In Roman mythology, he wears shining armor, and soldiers "rush on glorious death"[1] when they see that they will die on Mars's field of battle. His bird is the vulture, a bird of death.

Everything related to war can be found within the context of Mars. The sounds of war, the clothes of war, the qualities of war are all part of his character. Anything that is not war is not part of him. He contains none of the realistic ambivalences

[175]

about war and peace. There is no merriment in him, no uncertainties, no contradictions.

We might draw a continuum to show the relationship between the symbolic and the realistic characters.

One- dimensional symbolic character		Multi- dimensional character

If you placed Mars on the continuum, he would be a one-dimensional symbolic character. There are any number of realistic multidimensional characters that you can place at the other end of the continuum—Rick from *Casablanca*, Scarlett O'Hara, Shane, or Rose from *The African Queen*.

As you rank characters from one- to multidimensional, you can find other characters that fall somewhere in between.

The Stepford Wives are symbolic characters, representing the perfect wife. Everything associated with that concept is part of their makeup, including compliance to their husbands, and a commitment to a clean home, good food, and happy children. They are not given any characteristics that are not related to this role, nor is any of the imperfect reality of true-life wifehood allowed to creep into their personalities.

Other examples are the Common Man in *A Man for All Seasons* by Robert Bolt, and Everyman in the medieval play of the same name, who represent the ordinariness of people.

Many villains, as well as many superheroes, also are symbolic characters. The Joker from *Batman* represents evil, while Superman stands for "truth, justice, and the American way of life."

The creators of symbolic characters purposely do not add a great many details—just enough to communicate the idea.

When you place these characters on the continuum, you

may decide that Clark Kent and Bruce Wayne are purposely more dimensional than their Superman and Batman personas, but purposely less dimensional than characters such as Rick, Scarlett, Shane, or Rose. The order might look like this:

One-dimensional symbolic character				Multi-dimensional character
Mars	Stepford Wives	Superman	Clark Kent	Scarlett
	Everyman	Batman	Bruce Wayne	Rick
		Joker		Shane
				Rose

EXERCISE: Create a character who represents Justice. Begin by listing the qualities of justice. A partial list might include fairness, neutrality, being color blind and gender blind, a sense of both the letter and spirit of the law. You should be able to come up with twenty to fifty characteristics of Justice. To further develop this idea, think about Justice's parents. Perhaps one is a lawyer, representing Legality, and another is a philosopher, representing Wisdom. If you are creating a god or goddess character, you could stop here.

Now begin to give this character more dimensionality. Add related qualities that are not contradictory. Compassion, wisdom, insight, and the ability to negotiate are all possibilities.

Think about the difference between Justice as a symbolic character versus a realistic character in which justice might be a dominant quality, but the character would also contain the contradictions and ambivalences and paradoxes that are part of the fully dimensional person.

Symbolic characters, conveying one clear idea, can be helpful to express the theme of your story. Care must be taken, however, that their limitations don't make them seem like cardboard characters.

THE NONHUMAN CHARACTER

Most of us grew up reading about such nonhuman characters as Black Beauty, Lassie, Charlotte in *Charlotte's Web*, Bambi, Dumbo, or the Black Stallion. But nonhuman characters are not limited to children's stories. As adults, we may be fascinated by George Orwell's *Animal Farm*, or Caliban in *The Tempest*, or Harvey from the play of the same name.

Occasionally nonhuman characters are simply human characters with a bark, a bite, or a fluffy tail. They are anthropomorphic animals. Although the characters in *Animal Farm* are certainly not as dimensional as human characters, they purposefully are meant to remind us of humans. We might say they are humans in pigskin.

The creation of a nonhuman character may begin by emphasizing the animal's human side. Lassie is very loyal and gentle. Rin Tin Tin is very smart. Napoleon, the pig in *Animal Farm*, manipulates and tyrannizes others. But these qualities can do only so much for the characters. Simply watching a smart dog week after week or reading about a gentle horse is not going to be satisfying. A different approach is needed to create most workable nonhuman characters.

A human character achieves dimensionality by adding to, and emphasizing, its human characteristics. But emphasizing the nonhuman aspects of a character will rarely strengthen a nonhuman character. Emphasizing a dog's doglike characteristics (such as a louder bark or running faster to the food dish) is not going to make the dog more endearing to humans.

So a personality for the character needs to be created. A process for achieving this identity might include:

1. carefully choosing one or two attributes that will begin to define the identify of the character

2. emphasizing the associations that the audience brings to the character in order to expand on this identity
3. creating a strong context to deepen the character

Realistic characters are difficult to categorize compared to the clarity of nonhuman characters. Realistic characters may be loyal, but under certain situations, a threat to their survival could weaken their loyalty. They may be optimistic in outlook, but a tragic situation could change their viewpoint.

The nonhuman character, on the other hand, has clearly defined attributes that never change. Although these attributes may be based on human qualities, they won't have the shading, or the variety, that human characters have. Lassie will always be loyal, Rin Tin Tin will always be smart.

Al Burton, producer of the new "Lassie" series, says: "I would like to think that there is a constancy in Lassie that is rare within humans. The constancy is protective, loyal, trustworthy, courageous, a security blanket for a child."

These attributes, by themselves, will not give the characters enough variety and interest. Audiences need to project associations on to them. How do associations work? Let's look at the method used by the advertising industry to create a character for products such as cars, vegetables, or beers.

Michael Gill, vice president at the J. Walter Thompson advertising agency, explains their method of creating brand identity, which can also be used to create character identity: "Most consumers cannot tell the difference between beers, or washing detergents, or even Pepsi or Coke. So the job of the ad is to make it clear that this is a brand with a personality and an identity. It's similar to the brand on cattle—you see that brand and get an instant flash of recognition because that brand is used to differentiate cattle that all look alike. So Mercedes becomes the car of engineering, Ford stands for quality. Certain trucks stand for power and toughness. This nonhuman character—whether a car or a computer—becomes a personification of certain qualities. By associating the car with the quality, you get the rub-off, or the halo effect."

In advertising, this halo effect causes the consumer to want to buy the product. When applied to the creation of nonhuman characters, it increases the feeling of identity between the audience and the characters.

Sometimes the personality of the character in an ad comes from analyzing the properties of the product. The Pillsbury Doughboy makes one think of the way that dough is kneaded and rises. Snap, Crackle, and Pop, as everyone knows, come from the sounds of Kellogg's Rice Krispies. Spuds MacKenzie capitalizes on our associations with dogs as best friends, and in this case, a feisty and fun party animal.

At other times, the character identity comes from the added associations. The dancing raisins that advertise California Raisins have little to do with the properties of raisins. The creators didn't emphasize their wrinkles, or their small size, or their health properties. A greater leap was made. Seth Werner, who created the California Raisins, explains the beginning of that idea:

"The client had said to us, 'I'd like a celebrity campaign because I'd like my campaign to be bigger than just raisins. I figure a celebrity will give it personality and give it bigger presence than we can give with our product alone.' We said we thought we could make a celebrity out of the raisins themselves by giving them a personality. Our original idea (with my partner Dexter Fedor) was to have a bunch of raisins dance to 'I Heard It Through the Grapevine.' And then we started to think about what the raisins would look like. We decided that we wanted the raisins to be cool and a bit intimidating. In contrast, other snack foods would be less cool, less hip. We began creating a relationship between the raisins and other characters—such as the potato chips that wilt, the candy bars that melt, or gum that gets his shoe stuck to the table. And while the raisins were dressed in high-top sneakers with the laces untied and sunglasses, looking cool, the pretzels had wing-tipped shoes, a candy bar had desert boots—anything that would look less hip by comparison.

"We wanted the consumer to believe in the realism of these characters. It had to be anchored in reality or else you didn't buy it. That meant we had to create, not only the broad strokes, but also the subtleties and little touches that make it special."

All of these characters achieve their personality through associations. We bring certain feelings to the viewing of the character, and the character exemplifies these feelings. These associations can be strengthened by clarifying the character's context.

Lassie is defined by the family context. She exists in relationship. Steve Stark, the coproducer of the "Lassie" series, says, "We consider the dog as part of the family. She's really a best friend to the family, a best friend to the son. The new 'Lassie' series is not a kids' show, it's a family show. Lassie complements that by being part of the family, so when she's sick, our family's at her side; and when the family's sick, Lassie's at their side—just like a real family. Rin Tin Tin was the rescuer, Lassie is the confidante and the friend."

Producer Al Burton says, "The family context is a carryover from the old show, and emphasized in this series. We've added a girl to the show who also relates to Lassie. The value of Lassie to the family is that Lassie knows that she's needed. The family doesn't make a lot of moves without the audience feeling, 'Oh, boy, I'm glad they have Lassie.' Lassie is a much more sensitive animal than Rin Tin Tin, more relational, she seems to be automatically tuned in to the spirits of her family.

"Lassie is a wonderful companion and a wonderful friend, and in this age of bad relationships—and I think we do live in an age of bad relationships, especially among humans—it's great to have a dog to provide that tranquil relationship that one never gets anymore."

Compare the context of Lassie with the context of another nonhuman character, King Kong. He comes from the South

Seas, from a context that is primitive, dark, mysterious, and terrifying. The associations that come with him include vague knowledge of ancient religious rituals, human sacrifice, and a dark unrepressed sexuality. His origins are unknown, and what it takes to appease him is still somewhat mysterious. We are more frightened of King Kong because we bring to his character our own fear of the unknown.

EXERCISE: Using the process of choosing an attribute, expanding through associations, and clarifying context, create a strange, scaly creature from another planet. What qualities will you give it? Will you emphasize defensiveness, fear, intelligent manipulation? Or will you emphasize compassion, companionship, and lovability?

What associations do you bring to this character? The associations will change, depending on whether you emphasize negative or positive humanlike attributes.

What would its context be? Does it live deep within the earth, emphasizing a primitive, dark context? Does it come from the sky, emphasizing an otherworldly, or perhaps even a lighthearted context? Does it live upon the earth, which could make it more relational?

THE FANTASY CHARACTER

Fantasy characters live in a romantic, magical, strange world, inhabited by such unusual creatures as leprechauns, giants, goblins, trolls, and witches. There may be evil and darkness, but it's never ultimate. The characters may be dangerous, but not horrifying. They may be mischievous, but good will always triumph. Fantasy characters may even be redeemed in the end.

Characters within this magical context have a limited number of qualities. Sometimes they are defined by physical exaggeration, oversized like Paul Bunyan or diminutive like the Lilliputians in *Gulliver's Travels.*

Others are defined by their magical powers—Merlin the magician in the King Arthur legend or the Wicked Witch of the West in *The Wizard of Oz.*

Some are defined by being supergood, or superresourceful, or superbad. Almost all of the heroines, heroes, and villains in fairy tales answer to this description.

Although most fantasy characters are rooted in the fairy tale and the folk tale, new ones have been created. Some of these include the mermaid in *Splash,* the boy-man in *Big,* the Anterians in *Cocoon.*

In the television series "Beauty and the Beast," a fantasy character, Vincent, is paired with a realistic character, Catherine. Vincent's context—underground, earthy, primitive, always looking up to the light—contrasts with that of Catherine in her modern, high-rise apartment building. As a realistic character, she has a much fuller range of emotions to draw upon. She can be depressed, sad, frenetic, overworked, as well as loving, kind, understanding, and compassionate.

Vincent's qualities are more limited. He is not simply a realistic character wearing a lion's head. He remains within the confines of fantasy. Although deformed in appearance, Vincent's qualities are positive. He's kind, compassionate, caring. There is, at times, a sense of yearning, but this never compromises the goodness of his soul. Indeed, goodness is his defining characteristic. The style of the show is romantic, and Vincent is heroic—making it a modern fairy tale.

In advertising, one of the most successful fantasy characters is the Jolly Green Giant. The story of his creation shows how carefully choosing specific attributes can produce a clear and memorable character.

In 1924, a new brand of a larger sweet pea was marketed and called the "Green Giant." The Leo Burnett Agency was hired to develop the character. Many of their decisions reflected the desire to create a fantasy character. They began to develop the

[183]

positive context of the giant by placing him in a Green Valley and by having him carry associations of health and plenty.

Huntley Baldwin from the Leo Burnett Agency writes: "Deep down, at the heart of what we feel about food, is survival. In almost every primitive culture, great gods guided the hunt and guaranteed the harvest. A pantheon of gods made sure everything was plentiful, fresh, and wholesome. The Green Giant is a direct descendant of such gods. As with most fantasy characters, there are some details known about him. He lives in a valley where all good things come from. He guides the destinies of those who live and work there. He personally tends to every detail, from seed to harvest to packing."

Certain specific qualities were given to him to expand his character. "The Green Giant is the 'star' of the commercial," Baldwin continues, "but visually he plays a very supporting role. He is more a presence to be felt than a character to be seen. He is serious but not stuffy. He is friendly and warm (hence the 'ho-ho-ho'). But obscurity contributes to his fantasy. He is what everybody imagines him to be, not what one artist or cameraman reveals him to be."

Baldwin emphasizes that the giant needs to stay in a fantasy context. In one ad they placed the Green Giant among real people. It didn't work. "Real people can destroy the mood and the fantasy by reminding us the Giant is make-believe. The fantasy gives people permission to 'believe' what might otherwise be rejected as pure exaggeration. Animation extends the fantasy and allows the viewer to deal with the stories on a symbolic rather than a rational level."[2]

THE MYTHIC CHARACTER

Each of the three types of nonreal characters we've discussed have emphasized attributes, context, and/or associations. Creating the mythic character uses these same elements, but adds one other: an understanding of the audience.

The difference between an ordinary story and a myth depends on how the audience views it. Most fiction moves us in some way, whether to tears, laughter, or understanding. But with most good films and novels, once we finish watching or reading, the experience is over. Perhaps we'll remember a scene or a character for some time, but we don't continue to experience it.

When we finish reading or watching a mythic story, however, we add a reflective process to the experience. The scene or character comes back to haunt us. It doesn't let us go. A mythic story represents the meaning in our own lives. It conveys a story that can help us to better understand our own existence, our own values, our own yearnings. Many of us watch the movie or read the novel and project our own personal story on to the one being told.

Sometimes myths and mythic characters encourage us, motivate us, or push us into new behaviors or new understandings. We become, in a sense, bigger people as we identify with the heroic in the mythic characters.

Mythic stories are usually hero stories, containing a heroic figure who overcomes obstacles that stand in the way of his quest for a goal or treasure. As a rule, the hero is transformed in the course of his journey. As we watch the story unfold, we may think of our own heroic journeys. It might be the obstacles the writer has to overcome to sell that script or novel, or the problems encountered in a search for a fulfilling love, job, or life-style. The journey of the story may also remind us of our own inner journeys, as we seek value and meaning in our lives.

Many films contain mythic elements, such as a heroic character who overcomes obstacles on a journey, but if it does not engender reflection or identification, it will not be a true myth. The test is what the audience projects on to the story, and whether the story and characters help them to understand their own lives on a deeper level.

For instance, the newest Indiana Jones film, *Indiana Jones and the Last Crusade*, contains a larger-than-life hero who overcomes all manner of obstacles as he searches for the Holy Grail. To outward appearances, this would seem to be a myth since it contains most of the required elements.

Looking at the film in more depth, let's ask some mythic questions: Is Indiana's journey to find the Holy Grail similar to our own journeys toward fulfillment? Does his story encourage us to meet the obstacles in our own lives? Does the film bring us into a deeper relationship with our own personal stories?

For most members of the audience, the answer to these questions would probably be no. This does not detract from the fun or adventure of the film—but it does mean it probably is not operating as a myth.

You could ask these same questions of other films that have been called mythic, such as *E.T.*, *Close Encounters of the Third Kind*, *Blade Runner*, *Star Wars*, or *Robocop*.

Let's look at another character, one of the most successful in advertising, who is considered to be a mythic character—the Marlboro Man.

"In advertising, as in most fiction," says Michael Gill of J. Walter Thompson, "you need to tap into the subconscious of your audience. The Marlboro Man seemed to have done that. In Joseph Campbell's study of myth, he mentions that as long as humans and horses have been around there's a myth of the man on horseback. Usually this man is a great king, a god, a knight, or a warrior. With the Marlboro Man, of course, this man is the symbol of the West—the cowboy. People respect and idolize this person. When people smoke or drink they're not doing it casually, they're doing it to be associated with something that improves their feeling about themselves.

"The more realized the character is, the more people can relate to and like the character. In the Marlboro ad there's the mustache, the tattoo, and a white hat. A black hat would make a different statement. Usually he's mounted on a horse in wide open spaces, not towns. Towns are evil and risky and dangerous. Country is good. We always picture him in beautiful surroundings and with beautiful animals—an animal is the primal expression of freedom and indulgence and enjoyment. Fresh air and healthiness are very important. There's a feeling of confidence—that he's in charge. He's always either alone or, sometimes, with other men. But he's never with women—that's not part of the myth. Tapping into this mythic dimension in advertising is very rare—but the Marlboro Man seems to have done just that."

Most consumers of Marlboros have probably spent little time outside of a city, and may have never ridden a horse. But they project meaning on to the Marlboro Man. He stands for their desire for fresh air and open spaces, for their sense of confidence in themselves.

A case might be made that Vincent, in "Beauty and the Beast," is both a fantasy and a mythic character. Superman also could be considered a mythic character. Batman seems to be mythic as well, since the Batman story and character says something about the darkness and psychoses of our society.

Michael Besman, senior vice-president of production at Guber-Peters Entertainment, tells about the development of the character of Batman: "Batman is the quiet avenger. He's like Robocop. Bruce Wayne is the millionaire, the character with a split personality. Troubled by the death of his parents, he's out to avenge it. He's the uncomfortable one, having been brought up in the limelight as the wealthy heir. He's forced to deal with the press and forced to communicate with the public. As Batman, he doesn't have to mask his anger, he's able to release it. Bruce Wayne has to live in the world. He has an identity. Batman does not."

In a sense, Bruce Wayne had to deal with his human identity. He is a realistic character who chooses to become nonrealistic because it's simpler and more direct. By losing his dimensionality, he also is able to lose the pain of his humanity, which is so difficult to deal with. Bruce Wayne created Batman because he wishes that Batman would have been there to save his parents.

Besman contrasts the difference between the characters of

Superman and Batman: "Clark Kent is very much aware of his secret identity. When he came to earth, he grew into the role of Superhero, almost as an extension of his superpowers. But Batman evolves from pain, anger, and a need to express it.

"The audience reaction is very different to each character. I was a huge fan of the Superman comic books. I remembered thinking it would be great to actually have a Superman. It's almost like knowing God exists. It's security. I didn't want to *be* Superman. I'd like to hang out with him. Batman, however, is an uphill climb. He had to go through so much. There's more of an emotional connection. He's like us, less magical than Superman. Superman is very white bread. Batman is the other side of the coin."

The context of Batman also determines the character. In some of these comic-book heroes, the context is very dark. Besman continues: "This was a realistic, gritty, dark, and psychological rendering of Gotham City. It's an exaggeration of a place so the audience can fully grasp what compels a man to become a Batman."

A recent box-office smash features another mythic character, the Phantom of the Opera, who symbolizes the wounded victim. James Dearden, who wrote a movie script for this story, confronted how to make this character mythic. "In the script, what I tried to do was to create a phantom. But how do you try to write a guy who is hideously disfigured, and lives in a subterranean cave all his life and at the same time has a beautiful soul, and is capable of feeling love? Obviously that is not a real character, because a real character in those circumstances would be smelly and disfigured and psychologically twisted. Yet what we've got is based on the myth. I think we managed to create a character that was, in the context of the movie, consistent, who was a symbolic character you could believe in. The starting point in his creation is the value or idea. The idea in that instance is this hideously maimed outcast with the most beautiful, generous soul inside of him. 'Beauty and the Beast' was my paradigm for the Phantom."

Mythic characters tend to have certain specific qualities. They are usually heroic. Much is demanded of them, and they are able to meet the challenge. In the course of the story, mythic characters change, becoming stronger or wiser. The mythic figure often has a mysterious or dark past. There's a sense of some backstory that may not be revealed to the audience, although it may be implied.

Sometimes the writer (and the character) knows the past, but deliberately keeps it a secret because it is too painful to mention. The character may be unable to deal with it, and not want to talk about it. The backstory in this case is an essential part of the character, but because it's mysterious, audiences create their own interpretation of what happened. Shane, who partly stands for the myth of the Old West, could fit into this category.

Sometimes the past is known, or revealed during the story. The terrible deed that has motivated and obsessed Batman for his entire life touches on our own understanding of the power of revenge and obsession.

Every age creates new mythic stories that help us understand our lives. In the 1930s, Charlie Chaplin in *Modern Times* expressed the overwhelming helplessness that many feel in an overly industrialized society. More recently, *Blade Runner* showed us the natural consequences of continued corruption and overpopulation. Oliver Stone explored mythic characters in *Wall Street*'s tale of greed, and in *Platoon*'s story about good and evil and innocence lost. *Field of Dreams* explored our nostalgia for the past and for resolution, and *Sea of Love* and *Fatal Attraction* explored loneliness and the inherent danger in many modern relationships.

Mythic characters can be difficult to create. They need enough dimensionality to seem like real human beings, yet there has to be a sense of mystery, and some lack of specificity to enable them to represent not just a person, but a certain idea. They are both human and symbolic, with neither one overbalancing the other.

The ultimate test of a myth is whether it speaks to the audience's lives. Still, bringing in some mythic dimensions can deepen characters and strengthen the connections between their story and that of the audience.[3]

In the seminar with the staff of "MacGyver," mentioned previously, we discussed ways to add mythic dimensions to his character. The ABC network executive at the meeting, William Campbell III, thought it very important that MacGyver remained somewhat mysterious in order to be heroic. At the same time, the strength of the show came from the combination of action, intelligence, and emotions. I suggested that we might be talking about a new kind of hero and by brainstorming the character from a mythic perspective, we might be able to expand his character and the relationship that the audience has to him.

The definition of *hero* changes from age to age, but it changes very slowly. Heroes have been defined as warriors, conquerors, competitors—as men of action. Certainly MacGyver is a man of action. But he is a different type of hero. He responds nonviolently and noncompetitively to situations. The hero of the past set out to conquer the wilderness; MacGyver wants to protect the earth. The hero of the past was a rugged individualist; MacGyver is a humanist and team player. He could be a new kind of hero for today's youth. At a time when many young people withdraw into drugs, depression, and a sense of powerlessness, MacGyver represents alternative responses and behaviors.

Expanding the character of MacGyver could take two different directions. If the producers wanted to make him more mythic, they could create more stories about the important issues of our age—from corruption to ecology to genetic engineering—showing this new hero responding to these issues and finding nonviolent solutions.

To add to the mythic dimensions, the producers could decide to capitalize on something mysterious or unresolved from his past. This would enable audiences to project their own interpretations of his backstory on to the character.

However, since the strength of the character (and the actor) comes to a great extent through his ability to convey emotions and caring, and through his dimensionality (qualities that are not always found in mythic characters), trying to make him a classic mythic hero might be a mistake. MacGyver is a clear emotional character, without real mysteries in his past.

Instead, one could capitalize on his context in a technological society, his ability to overcome obstacles, and on some of his larger-than-life qualities. If the context and associations were expanded, the relationship with the audience might be thought through in mythic terms, without compromising his human, dimensional qualities.

A CASE STUDY:
THE NEVERENDING STORY II

In spring 1989, I consulted on the The Neverending Story II (the sequel) that was filmed that summer (and due to be released in fall 1990). The story itself begins with the realistic characters of Bastian and his father, and then moves to the fantasy world of Fantasia, where we encounter fantasy characters who are nonhuman, symbolic, and/or mythic characters. In this film, most characters fit into more than one category.

Some of the nonhuman characters are the Wambos, Wind Bride, Lava Man, Mud Wart, the two-faced Nimbly, and Falkor the dragon and Rockbiter, who were also in Part One.

Of these, the Wambos, Wind Bride, Lava Man, and Mud Wart are also symbolic characters.

Karin Howard, the writer, explains how she created them: "Some of these characters were derived from the book. The Wambos are the creatures that help storm the castle. The summer that I thought of them was the summer you saw

Rambo posters wherever you looked. Since their function is similar, instead of calling them Rambo, I called them Wambos. I thought about what makes up an army—such as the noise and the dust—so these creatures create the illusion of battle without really doing anything more than making noise and smoke and dust.

"The characters from the Ship of Secret Plots—Earth, Air, Wind, and Lava—were created for exposition. In Part One, there was a patriarch who carried out this function. But a patriarch can be philosophical and talky, and I wanted a more visual expression. These emissaries—messengers—explain the situation to Bastian. I took the idea for them from earth, wind, and fire, but made them the mud creature, the wind creature, the fire creature. To expand their characters, I gave them names. Once I had names, I began to think of associations with those names. The instrument creature sounded a little shrill and spinsterish, so I made her into an instrument spinster who represented sound. And the Mud Wart is obviously something that grunts and who represents earth. The Lava Man is fire, and the Wind Bride is the wind.

"In the book, there's a one-paragraph description about Nimblies—the messengers bearing a certain resemblance to a rabbit. These creatures are among the swiftest runners in Fantasia. I took that idea and created one character called Nimbly who would have running shoes, sneakers, a baseball cap. I realized that if he were running so fast, he would probably have awkward landings; perhaps he'd somersault. I gave him a function—that he was in the service of the witch, probably a spy. And I thought of the word *turncoat*. So the production department had to physically create a character that communicated *turncoat*. We physicalized it by seeing him as a creature that could fold his feathers back—showing his bad side when he's with the witch, but when he's with Bastian and Atreyu—the good guys—he moves his feathers forward and shows his good side.

"Nimbly works with Three-Face, the scrupulous scientist

who's willing to be the perfect tool. He's a combination of a crazy technician, a Frankenstein, and the gatekeeper in the city of the Old Empress.

"I originally had him with a resin body—you could see all the pipes going through this body so he was more of a robot. Now he's more of a magician in a white coat with three eyes.

"My favorite creature in Part One was Rockbiter. He's a big clunky creature with little bitty eyes and a funny pointed head who eats rocks. Out of a brainstorming meeting we came up with the baby, Rockbiter, Jr. In Part One, Fantasia was threatened by the Nothing, but in Part Two it's threatened by the Emptiness. Junior is hungry, since the rocks in Fantasia were empty. So his function advanced the theme of the Emptiness.

"Falkor the dragon came already very well defined from Part One. He's the director's and marketing people's favorite. Falkor is the most relational character, the best friend. He has a wonderful understanding of human nature and a fine sense of humor, because he understands the foibles of human nature and will always take the positive point of view."

These nonhuman characters all had different functions. Nimbly and the Wambos had a story function, the Creatures were there to give exposition, and the Rockbiters advanced the theme.

In the film, there are a number of human characters. Bastian and his father are realistic characters from earth, the other characters are fantasy characters from Fantasia. Bastian and the fantasy characters of Xayide the witch, the Child-like Empress, Atreyu, the warrior from Fantasia are also mythic characters, taking part in the journey to save Fantasia from the Emptiness.

Karin continues: "Bastian is the human character, and therefore the one with the most free will and the most unpredictability. He can make all the wrong or all the right choices. He and his father are the most dimensional characters.

"Atreyu, the warrior from Fantasia, was a problem because he can be boring, too 'goody-goody.' In the book, Atreyu was

CREATING UNFORGETTABLE CHARACTERS

jealous of Bastian; but for the film, the producers felt that the boys needed to be buddies. We did shade in some jealousy for interest, but this relationship is only a C story so it was important that it not dominate the film.

"Xayide is the witch of Fantasia. I wanted her sexy. I wanted her to be a very willful woman and very hip, singing in her throne room and kicking off her shoes, and being very impatient when things aren't going her way. The Child-like Empress was a goody-goody and here was this sexpot Xayide who finally said, 'This is enough and it's my time to shine, and I want to take over Fantasia and by golly I'm going to do it' and was very upset when all her tanks and her giants would malfunction. So I created a lot of humor out of things malfunctioning and Xayide just going bananas when things weren't going her way. Xayide is a representative of the Emptiness, and is a character who's against stories and imagination.

"The Child-like Empress was another important fantasy character. I spent the least amount of time on developing her because she was clearly defined in Part One, and only had a one-day shooting role. She's this beautiful young girl with this lovely little voice—and she's too good for words. So you want to create these wonderful words and put them in her mouth. She doesn't know good or evil. All are equal before her, she doesn't judge. In German, we would say she's *kitschig*, but for some reason that works with her."

APPLICATION

If your script contains nonrealistic characters, ask yourself:

- What idea is being communicated by this character?
- What associations come to mind with this idea? Have I brainstormed these associations, to make sure that they are consistent with the character I want to create?

- What is the context of my character? If I change or expand the context, will that help strengthen the character?
- How does the character relate to the universal stories of the audience? If my character is mythic, have I explored the various dimensions of the myth to make sure it is clear?

SUMMARY

Nonrealistic characters are determined by four different criteria: To what extent do they exemplify an idea? How does the context help define the character? What associations does the audience bring to the character? And does this character help the audience understand the meaning in their own lives, in their own individual stories?

Nonrealistic characters have been successful in novels and stories (*Black Beauty*, Grimm's and Andersen's fairy tales, Charlotte in *Charlotte's Web*), in films (*E.T.*, *King Kong*, *Close Encounters of the Third Kind*), and in television series ("Alf," "Lassie," "Rin Tin Tin"). The recent box-office hits of *Batman*, *Superman*, *Turner and Hooch*, and *The Phantom of the Opera* have created more of a market and more of a need for writers to be able to write the nonrealistic character.

9

Beyond Stereotyping

Fiction can be powerful. Characters have the potential to affect our lives on many levels. They can inspire us, motivate behavior, help us understand ourselves and others, expand our insight into human nature, and even be role models—leading us to new decisions about our lives.

But just as characters can have a positive influence, they can also affect us negatively. There is strong evidence that criminal behavior has, at times, been copied from television shows. A number of studies have inferred a relationship between violence on television and violence among children and adults. And there is evidence that stereotyping can cause audiences to have a negative impression of an entire group of people. As a writer creating dimensional characters, understanding stereotyping and breaking stereotypes is essential.

We might define a stereotype as the continual portrayal of a group of people with the same narrow set of characteristics. Usually a stereotype is negative. It shows a cultural bias toward the characteristics of one's own culture, painting characters outside that culture in limiting, and sometimes, dehumanizing ways.

Who gets stereotyped? Anyone who is different from us. Anyone we don't understand. This can include ethnic minorities, such as blacks, Asians, Hispanics, and Native Americans, if you're a white writer; or it can include whites, if you're a minority writer. People with physical disabilities are often stereotyped, as well as the developmentally disabled, the emotionally disturbed, the mentally ill.

Religious groups are often stereotyped, whether Muslims, Catholics, Jews, Fundamentalists, mainline Protestants, Hindus, or Buddhists.

The opposite sex can be stereotyped, whether female or male. People with sexual orientations different from our own get stereotyped—gays, lesbians, even occasionally heterosexuals.

People who are older or younger than we are often are stereotyped, as are those who come from another culture.

Stereotypes vary for different groups. Women and minorities are often portrayed as victims. In many films, particularly, they tend to be expendable. Either they're the first ones to die or they're the ones who need rescuing by the white male.

People with disabilities are often portrayed as the "handicapped horror," with a certain deformity of the body symbolizing a deformity of the soul. Or they are portrayed as the pitiful victim, or else as the Supercrip, a term sometimes used by people with disabilities to connote the Superman or Superwoman who performs tremendous feats and is able to overcome the disability through miraculous means.

Blacks are often portrayed as comical, or the butt of the joke, or as perpetrators of crimes. Asian women will often be portrayed as the exotic-erotic, the men as mindless hordes, or sometimes, even as the model minority—well off and well behaved. Although the latter may not seem negative, it is limiting and stereotypical since it doesn't recognize that Asians are affected by the same problems as any other group.

Think how often the Native Americans have been portrayed as the bloodthirsty savages or the drunken, cowardly outlaws. And how often Hispanics are portrayed as gang members or bandits, or as Luis Valdez says, "The assumption is that Hispanic stories only take place in the Southwest behind adobe walls and under a tile roof."[1]

Even the white male has not escaped stereotyping. An emphasis on the man of action, whether the strong silent type or the supermacho, denies a whole group of men images that reflect their identity. Men who are househusbands, massage therapists, or schoolteachers can feel their contributions as nurturers devalued. The thinking man or the man of compassion rarely sees images that reflect his reality.

Most groups, from secretaries to blondes to basketball players to WASPS to Vietnam vets to lawyers, have at one time or another been portrayed in a stereotypical manner. Very few groups have been immune from our natural desire to simplify complex human characters. No one is exempt.

A *character type* is not the same as a stereotype. The doddering father or the braggadocio soldier are character types, not stereotypes, because the portrayal is balanced with other images of fathers and soldiers. Readers and audiences do not form the conclusion that "all fathers are doddering" or "all soldiers are braggadocio" as a result of this image. The character type doesn't suggest that everyone in a certain group (such as fathers) has the same characteristic (doddering). The stereotype does.

MOVING BEYOND THE STEREOTYPE

In spite of the good intentions of many writers, fictional characters are predominantly white and do not accurately portray reality. The population of the United States consists of about 12 percent blacks, 8.2 percent Hispanics, 2.1 percent Asians, and 2 percent Native Americans, and 20 percent of all people have a disabling condition—but most fiction portrays quite a different reality.

In a recent analysis of television shows, a study by the U.S.

Civil Rights Commission found that although 39.9 percent of the U.S. population is made up of white males, white males make up 62.2 percent of all characters on television.

Whereas 41.6 percent of the U.S. population consists of white females, and 9.6 percent of the population consists of minority females, television drama vastly underrepresents them. In the analysis, 24.1 percent of all television characters were white females, and only 3.6 percent were minority females.[2]

In a country where 95 percent of all women work outside the home during their lifetime, the "woman in the home" stereotype is no longer true. In a country where 40 percent of theology and law students are women, it's a misrepresentation to only occasionally portray women as lawyers or judges or ministers in films or on TV. In a country where women are pilots, mechanics, telephone repair people, and rabbis, an accurate portrayal of a society would show women characters in these roles. To only play the white male gender ideal in characters ignores the variety of people within our culture.

Such statistics can be helpful to a writer in deciding what kind of characters to add to a story. It's a good beginning point, even though the makeup of a society changes from city to city. If you want to truthfully represent reality in your San Francisco story, you will have a larger percentage of Asians and gays. If you're writing a story that takes place in Los Angeles, the number of Hispanics will be greater. And a story set in Detroit or Atlanta will have a larger percentage of blacks.

Moving beyond stereotyping means training our minds to see beyond white. The creation of characters is partly a retraining of our powers of observation. In any setting, we are trained to first see the prevailing group of people. For instance, if you had visited my hometown of Peshtigo, Wisconsin (population 2,504) in the 1950s, you could easily have stereotyped it as a white, middle-class, quiet community made up almost equally of Protestants and Catholics, with a few "We don't go to church" people.

If you took a closer look, you would begin to see diversity

within the community. In those years, Peshtigo had one Jewish family who owned the local appliance store, one family who had fled from Latvia after the war, some Mexicans who in the summer picked cucumbers for the nearby pickle factory, an occasional Menominee Indian from the nearby reservation who shopped at my father's drugstore, one small-statured person who helped children across the street after school, one mentally retarded fifth-grade girl, one eighth-grade girl who had lost an arm from cancer, four very rich families, and three very poor families.

A few years later, if you took another look at what seemed like a quiet town where nothing ever happened, you would see other details that broke the stereotype. These would include three bank robbers who were caught six hours after robbing the Peshtigo State Bank (they took the only dead-end road out of town!), and an antiwar activist minister who (to the chagrin of his congregation) led local protest marches during the Vietnam War. In recent years there has been the addition of three nationally renowned figures: the lawyer F. Lee Bailey, who has a second home in the neighboring town; Sergeant Medina, who was associated with the My Lai incident in Vietnam; and the mercenary Eugene Hasenfus.

As you may notice from the description of Peshtigo, many of these people are not defined by their ethnicity (the Jewish family, the Protestant) but by their role (owner of a store, antiwar minister).

As a beginning point, looking at the diversity within your own context can affirm the general research you have already done. Any of the people from your own background can serve as excellent models for minority characters.

Adding minorities to a novel or short story can be relatively easy: you just write them in. For dramatic writing, it may seem that adding an Indian doctor or a Korean mechanic is really a casting decision. Often it is—and the issue becomes complex because casting directors and producers don't often think about placing minorities in the story. But there are actions that a writer can take.

Shelley List, former supervising producer–head writer on "Cagney and Lacey," says: "Because I care about how minorities are portrayed, I generally will write in the addition of the minority. Instead of being general or leaving it up to the vagaries of the casting director, I'll specify that the school is made up of Asians and blacks and whites. Or I might mention the Hispanic Judge, the Black Engineer, or the Asian Anchorwoman. The network usually doesn't question it, or notice it. The script goes to the casting director, who simply follows the definitive descriptions."

Some of the most critically acclaimed performances of the last few years have come from members of minorities who played roles that were not "minority-specific"—that is, roles that could have been played by whites. The Eddie Murphy role in *Beverly Hills Cop* was originally written for Sylvester Stallone. The Lou Gossett role in *An Officer and a Gentleman* was written for a white. The Sigourney Weaver role in *Alien* was originally written for a man. Many of Whoopi Goldberg's recent roles were not minority-specific, and some of them were not even written for a woman. With each of these characters, the actor added something special to the role because of his or her own cultural background, although the role was not defined by gender or culture or ethnicity.

Most members of minorities prefer being cast in this way, rather than being the black playing a black, or a person with a disability playing a person with a disability.

EXERCISE: Imagine creating a scene in a hotel in a major U.S. city that is statistically representative of the types of people who would be staying there. What kind of black characters might you have? Hispanics? People with disabilities? What professions might these people be in? What would be their sex? Age? Religion?

HOW DO YOU DIMENSIONALIZE
THESE ROLES?

Writing a character from a culture other than one's own in-cludes, first, creating the character as fully human, with the full range of feelings and attitudes and actions of any other person, and, second, understanding the influence that the specific culture will have on the makeup of a character. As with any characters you create, a character from another culture will be both the same as and different from yourself.

To move beyond the stereotype demands a certain amount of specialized research from the writer. Sometimes the knowl-edge a writer brings from even the recent past is no longer relevant to the present. Women, men, people with disabil-ities, and ethnic minorities have all redefined themselves in the past few years, as they have insisted on their own rights within society. It is important to have some experience with the groups you are writing about—and/or to ask for ad-vice. A number of organizations, including the NAACP, Nos-otros (a Hispanic group), the Alliance of Gay and Lesbian Artists, Asian-Pacific Americans, and the California Gover-nor's Committee for the Employment of Disabled Persons, can be resources if you have questions or need advice, and most have people who can consult on portrayals within your story.

You might also ask someone from the minority group you're portraying to read your script or novel. For a woman writer, it can be helpful to have a man go over the material. Male writers can ask women to read their stories. Character details may be very subtle, and it often takes someone who understands the character from the inside out to clarify details, and to create a reality that rings true.

Some months ago, William Kelley (*Witness*) called me about a religious character he was creating. Knowing that I was a

Quaker, he wanted to check a few details about his Quaker female character. Those he mentioned seemed well researched and very astute. He then read me a prayer he had written for his character. I told him, "Bill, you've created a Methodist prayer, not a Quaker prayer." Our conversation affirmed the direction of his character, and also clarified one important detail.

EXERCISE: Imagine writing a funeral scene. What would it be like if it were a funeral from your own culture? Think about the funerals you've attended from other cultures. How do they vary? How would you go about finding out the difference between a Jewish funeral, a Southern black funeral, and a Quaker memorial service?

Think about the weddings you've attended. What are the differences between them? How did the various weddings express the cultural backgrounds of the bride and groom?

A CASE STUDY:
THE WOMEN IN FILM LUMINAS AWARDS

Many groups, recognizing the harm that stereotypes can do, have become increasingly vocal about the need to portray women and minorities more realistically.

In 1983, in an effort to change the way that women were depicted in the media, an international organization called Women in Film designed an award, the Luminas Award, to reward positive nonstereotypical portrayals of women. I was the chair of the committee, set up to create criteria that would help us identify stereotypes as well as positive female characters.

The criteria can be used to advantage by writers, producers, and directors to break through any stereotypes that are emerging in the characters they are working on.

Originally, there were eight criteria. In this case study,

I am focusing on five of the criteria that are most applicable to both women and minorities. (A list of all eight appears on pages 223–224.)

Nonstereotypical characters are multidimensional.

Stereotypical characters generally are one-dimensional. They are sexy, or violent, or greedy, or manipulative. Dimensional characters contain values and emotions and attitudes and paradoxes. Breaking a stereotype means humanizing the person to show the depth and breadth of the character.

Nonstereotypical characters are seen in a variety of social and personal roles and in a variety of contexts.

Often stereotypical characters are defined in limited roles and limited contexts. A woman might be seen simply as the boss's wife, or as a mother, a secretary, or a vice president. Dimensional characters play many roles and exist in a variety of contexts. They are not limited, but are both individual and relational people, and products of their culture and occupation, of their location and their history. Adding other roles and contexts will expand the character and break the stereotype.

Nonstereotypical characters reflect the range of age, race, socioeconomic class, physical appearance, and occupations present in society at large.

To break stereotypes, stories need to portray more truthfully the makeup of our society. In television, most women are young, beautiful, and rich, which belies the important contributions of women over forty, as well as the social reality that women earn less money than men. In most stories, minorities are relegated to only a few occupations and to a lower socioeconomic class, which misrepresents their influence and contributions. Understanding the statistical representation of the society of your story, and representing it realistically, will expand the palette of your story.

Nonstereotypical characters move the story through attitude, behavior, and inner purpose, thereby affecting the outcome.

Stereotypical characters are often reactive, rather than active. They are controlled by the story and are victims of the more powerful characters in the story. Dimensional characters, in contrast, are inner-directed rather than outer-directed. They influence the story, move the action, and affect the outcome. Giving characters intentionality will strengthen them, and move them from being victims to being powerful influences upon the story.

Nonstereotypical characters reflect their culture and provide new insights and new role models because of the influence of their background.

Many stereotypical characters are general characters. They will act just the same as the white male, even though their background has conditioned them to have other perspectives. Many times a woman or a member of a minority will have a different attitude toward a problem, or a different idea about how to resolve it, or will recommend another response. This new slant on a situation can add creative details and unusual twists to your story that you won't achieve by using only characters from one culture. Breaking stereotypes means recognizing the contributions that people from another cultural background can make. By valuing what they have to offer, characters outside your own culture can add color and texture and uniqueness to your stories.

The Luminas Award was first given in 1986. At this writing, it has been discontinued with some thoughts of reinstituting it at a later date. The criteria, however, continue to be used by some industry members in their own character creations.

APPLICATION

Think for a moment about the people you know who are black, Hispanic, Native American, Asian, etc. Think about how media usually portrays these people, and how that varies from your own experience. Are there any people in any of these groups you have never met? What do you *think* is true about these people? Try to find out the truth, particularly if you decide to use one of these ethnic groups within your story.

Apply the criteria from the case study to several films you've seen in the last year. Where is each film weak? Where is it strong? Where could it have been better *without* compromising its story?

Think about your hometown. What diversity was there among the people you knew growing up? Were there people from certain cultures with whom you had no contact? Did you have stereotypical ideas about these people? How did you begin to break those stereotypes?

Think about the context for the characters of your script. Have you explored the diversity within their particular location? Do you need to do further research about some of your people in order to portray them accurately? Who do you know within the minority group who could read your script and give suggestions as to how to further dimensionalize the character?

SUMMARY

Breaking stereotypes is not a process that the writer needs to do alone. All of the groups mentioned have printed material that can help give further understanding of specific minority characters. Most of them, too, have other resources available to the writer, such as people able to consult on portrayals within the script.

Adding positive depictions of women and minorities to your story can expand the palette of your story, and create stronger, clearer, and more dimensional characters.

10

~~~~~

Solving Character Problems

Writers get stuck—and characters get stuck. Sometimes ideas just don't come. Sometimes characters don't seem to go anywhere, and all the basic questions—What does the character want? Who is this character? What is he or she doing in the story?—don't seem to have any answers. For some writers, these moments fill them with dread. Others see them as simply part of the creative process.

Sometimes writers get stuck on characters simply because they've been overworking and are so exhausted that their minds don't function well.

Some character problems occur because the writer has not done enough research. If you don't understand the character's context, the character won't work.

Other problems occur because writers spend so much time writing, they've stopped living. Carl Sautter says, "You have to try to have a life. You have to realize that you're more than just a writer and that there is a world out there. Because if you're not in it, then you're not writing as well as you could be, because you're missing what is going on."

There's nothing unusual about confronting character problems. Every writer does it. Usually the problems fall into several different categories:

PROBLEMS WITH
UNLIKABLE CHARACTERS

When Judith Guest was writing *Ordinary People,* she had a difficult time understanding Beth. She says, "Beth works fine to define the plot and move the story. But for my own purposes as an author, she feels like a failure to me. There are too many people who say to me, 'I hated her.' And that seems to be the fault of the writer because I didn't intend for people to hate her except I think I hated her too at the beginning of the book. When I first started writing the book, I blamed her for what had happened to Conrad. The longer I wrote, the more complex the situation appeared to me and the less I blamed her. I decided not to go inside Beth's head because I was afraid I'd reveal how little I knew about her inner workings. At that time I told my friend and fellow novelist, Rebecca Hill, that I couldn't get inside this character and she said, 'I'll tell you why—you hate her and she isn't going to reveal herself to you.'

"Sometimes writers don't understand the character because the part that they hate is somehow a part of them. I think if you can join with that part of yourself that feels this way it will help you to get a handle on the character. I do think there's cruelty in all of us, stupidity, willfulness, all the character traits about yourself that you dislike, and you try to correct them in yourself and repress them, and believe that they don't exist. When you see them in other people it makes you furious. So I think maybe a way in is to accept these parts of yourself that you hate, and even love them in some way because they're part of you."

Robert Benton concurs. "There are characters that I knew I needed to write and I just couldn't write them because I didn't like them, and I had to go find some other character. There have also been times where I've written a character and I shouldn't have. It never works."

If a character is a reflection of your own shadow side, he or she might be difficult to like. By understanding and accepting your own psychology, you'll be more able to write characters you might consider negative.

PROBLEMS
WITH UNDERSTANDING THE CHARACTER

There are times when writers can't figure out their character. No matter how much work they've done, the character still eludes them. Frank Pierson recommends learning more about the character by creating scenes that will never appear in the script. "Maybe you don't know enough about the characters and how they relate to each other. . . . one way of dealing with it is to sit these people down in a situation which has nothing to do with the screenplay at all, e.g.: One of them orders a lunch and sends it back to the kitchen, which is very embarrassing to the other character. And what happens out of that? How do they talk about it? How do they argue about it? How do they fight? How would these characters change a tire on the Santa Monica Freeway in the rain? How would they get change for a $100 bill in Detroit after midnight? Write those scenes and you will teach yourself more about the characters than you will almost any other way."[1]

PROBLEMS
WITH VAGUE CHARACTERS

Characters, like people, are unique and detailed and specific. Sometimes characters don't work because they're too generalized and vague.

Robert Benton says, "Unless I'm careful I will find myself

writing characters that are general rather than specific. That is, they never rise above the needs of the plot. If characters are good, they will impose themselves upon the plot and force the plot to accommodate them. They're simply not tools of the plot or tools of a kind of moral concept that you want to get across. Sometimes I've made the character too consistent or sometimes I've made them comment on themselves, and sometimes I've made them abstract ideas. When that happens, I go back and throw the character out and begin to rethink it from the beginning. What I try to do most often is find somebody that I know, or have known, as a model for my character. If you take somebody that you know fairly well, you're bound to have certain insights into them. When it gets hard for me is when I write a character that's based on a movie character, a character from another movie. If I try to write a John Wayne character, as in *Rio Bravo,* it never works. I've tried it many times. The only time it works is when I take a character from my life and superimpose it over that character. I use certain people over and over—using different aspects of them. I've used my wife in twenty different ways in many of my scripts.

"During *Kramer vs. Kramer,* Dustin Hoffman taught me a lot about writing, so that every character at every moment must be specific. He really made me see as we worked on that picture, there was no moment that character had where he could afford to be general. He had to be specific and precise."

PROBLEMS WITH COMMERCIALITY

Most American producers and actors demand sympathetic and positive characters. This can create character problems, particularly when a writer has drawn a well-rounded, fascinating, but negative character that isn't workable for the American marketplace.

Kurt Luedtke says: "I'm having a problem with a character I'm writing now, but it's not because I'm blocked on the character. I know the character very well, maybe too well. But he's other than a commercial movie hero. If I didn't have to worry about that, I could do some interesting things with this character. But part of the job is trying to find a character that fifty million people are going to want to see."

In a case like this, the writer may need to rethink the character, or begin adding positive attributes to balance the flaws.

PROBLEMS WITH
SUPPORTING CHARACTERS

Sometimes a supporting character takes over the story. Writers have two different viewpoints about what to do when this happens. Dale Wasserman says, "That's trouble. Because if a supporting character starts to take over, I'd take it as something wrong with the story idea or structure. And that I hadn't thought it through well enough to begin with. That happens pretty often. It generally indicates that you have contrived rather than constructed your story. And in the process of contriving, characters were not in balance and did not serve the story in right proportions."

Sometimes, though, this can be an advantage. Robert Benton says, "In *Places in the Heart*, Edna Spalding took over the story. Originally the story was about bootleggers in Texas. Edna came into the movie as a minor character and she just pushed everybody away. When I love writing the most is when a character takes over. When I don't like writing is when I have to drag the character with me. That means I know I'm doing something wrong. Sometimes a character taking over can be the best thing for the story."

Some characters are too obedient. It's as if the writer is manipulating puppets, rather than entering into a dynamic relationship with the characters, allowing them also to have their say in the story.

Shelley Lowenkopf says, "One of the things to get a begin-ning writer to do is to back off and leave the characters room to expand in the story. Sometimes it's vital to a sense of ten-sion and suspense that the characters take on a life of their own."

STORY PROBLEMS
VS. CHARACTER PROBLEMS

Sometimes a character won't come alive because it's a story problem, not a character problem. Kurt Luedtke comments: "When there's a real problem with a character, the first thought I have is not to fix the character but to lose him. When you start trying to fix him, you can always do things to make a character more interesting, but it's pretty artificial when you do it. It's not hard to think of a behavior that they have, or a tic or a past or a dress or a style. I don't say that it doesn't work as a matter of entertainment, but it makes me restless. I think it's a little bit cheap to come up with expedient solutions when another character might start taking on a life and be much more inter-esting. I'd rather lose a character that refuses to come alive and try to find one that will.

"Maybe there's a very specific story reason why you can't lose the character, but the story can be rather malleable. And if the character who won't come alive seems to be needed from a story standpoint, you've probably uncovered a story flaw. It's not a character flaw, it's a problem in the story, because if that person's critical and the story's right, why wouldn't they come alive? My suspicion is that you're button-pushing the plot. You need someone to walk in, throw a switch, and get off, and you may think that it's a nice story move, but if it's not working, I'd look at the story first.

"If I can't get rid of the character, because I need him for story reasons to do this thing, my next thought would be, That's a fragile story that depends on a character that won't work to do something; let's look a little more. There's a problem that looks like a character problem, but it's really a story problem."

TECHNIQUES
FOR BREAKING THROUGH

Character problems are solvable. Experienced writers have many techniques that help them work through character blocks.

Gayle Stone: "Sometimes it helps to do a technique called 'free writing.' Basically, it's writing anything that you can about people that you know, people that you can imagine, scenes that you see, maybe just looking out your window and describing the view. This often helps you to begin making connections between what is coming out of your head and the solution to your plot, story, or character problem."

Shelley Lowenkopf: "When I'm stuck, I look at the hidden agenda of the major characters, what they really want. Discovering the hidden agenda helps me understand the character again."

Kurt Luedtke: "If you're stuck on a character, get somebody else to read the pages. They'll say, 'I don't understand why he or she does such and such,' which can jar your vision. It can knock you out of what you're thinking about.

"If you continue to have problems, 'What if' it for a while. 'What if this guy has no left foot?' 'What if something happened to this character when he or she was fifteen?'

"If you have a primary character that's not working, you've really got a problem. If you have a secondary character problem, you can more easily fix it. You might research it, or look for another character that can do the same sort of story things.

"If I had to pick one single thing to do, with primary characters or secondary characters, look at gender switch. It is incredible the number of things that will open up if you say, 'Well, if Dwayne is Susie . . .' There is a different set of attitudes and a new excitement to the characters because of the stereotypical and two-dimensional way in which we inevitably treat men and women."

Karin Howard: "Sometimes you have a name and nothing happens with it. I think names are very important. Many names have associations with them. Getting the right name and the right association can make your character come alive."

James Dearden: "If I were stuck, I'd just talk to my wife. It's a question of airing the problem and hitting the ball back and forth, and trying to talk through it. That's why there's such a thing as great editors in the lives of great writers. They send their manuscripts off to their editors and they come back with notes and hints and suggestions. Which doesn't mean the writer didn't know his job. It just means that he couldn't see the wood for the trees."

Getting perspective on a character problem helps the writer see that it need not be overwhelming. Character problems are a natural part of the creative process and are part of both character and writer finding their way.

A CASE STUDY:
DENYS FINCH-HATTON IN
OUT OF AFRICA

Occasionally, there are character problems that are never solved by the writer. This can happen with the best of writers. It is, perhaps, more difficult when one is writing a character based on a real-life person. Sometimes there is insufficient research material about the person. Sometimes there is not sufficient conflict or clear enough desires and goals to make the person a workable dramatic character. The solution to certain character problems will continue to elude the writer, no matter how skilled he or she is.

In 1985, *Out of Africa* won the Academy Award for Best Screenplay Adaptation, for Best Director, and for Best Picture.

Yet many critics felt that there was a flaw in the character realization of Denys Finch-Hatton. Kurt Luedtke, the writer, would agree.

I decided to use Finch-Hatton as a case study because the thinking that Kurt went through to resolve the problems that arose has much to say about the process of working through a character.

Kurt Luedtke: "Denys we never solved. The research was no help. He was a truly, deliberately elusive person who did not want to be known and took real steps not to be known. He tried to cover his tracks by telling all of his friends to read his letters and burn them. People have described him as similar to one of the African cats—like a leopard who moved only when there was a very specific reason. Even the natives didn't understand him. So I was never able to get anything very dramatic about him. Everything I knew about him tended to be negatives and I never found terrific ways to turn them into positives. It's an odd kind of writing problem. I think the truth about him is that he wanted very little and didn't want any appetite to control him. He was real rigorous about not wanting things. I never thought of terrifically interesting ways to dramatize 'not wanting.'

"I think if I had loosened up a bit, discarded some of what I knew about the real Finch-Hatton, I could have written a character that could say, 'I don't care about your mind or about any of this, we're a little short of women in this country and what I love about you is your mighty fine skin and that's all I want.' I could have written a character with a very specific set of attitudes that at least would give an actor a set of things to do that would be a bit more active.

"But, as a writer, I think it would have been very difficult to deal with a real character and have him say things that I knew were not true. I would have had some ethical problems with it. I would have felt a real encumbrance because I was working with true material and a literary figure that I happen to care a lot about. If I had to cheat like that, I just wouldn't make the picture. If we're going to do that, we may as well not call it *Out of Africa* and let's name her Shirley and name him Bill. I just don't think we should do *Out of Africa* if we aren't staying within the boundaries. If you're going to make it up, let's really make it up."

There are a number of qualities that a character must have to be intrinsically dramatic. One of these is *intentionality.* "What does the character want?" is a question asked by many producers and executives. For Denys, the answer seemed to be "Nothing."

Kurt continues, "I never knew the real Finch-Hatton, but from what little I know about him, I suspect and believe that he was a very contained man who didn't really want very much, who had what he wanted. He is an intrinsically undramatic character. You could do a movie just about his external acts, since he did have filmic adventures, but the inner qualities are unknown. To the extent that Finch-Hatton is interesting, it's Karen that makes him interesting. It's her appetite and her needs and her motivation and her situation. The fact of the matter is, if we were really willing to fictionalize Finch-Hatton, this Finch-Hatton character is not the man you would have made up with Karen Blixen. If you stayed with the truth, Bror is a lot more interesting. I could have written the whole movie about their marriage."

But the film focused on the love story. So Kurt tried to define Denys in other ways.

"We tried a little bit to suggest that by being so self-contained, he has a problem. There was a scene that was made up but not inconsistent with what may have been the case, when his good friend Berkeley Cole is dying. It's discovered that Berkeley Cole for a good number of years has maintained a relationship with a Somali woman. Denys is startled to discover this and he says, 'Why didn't you tell me?' and Berkeley says, 'I suppose I thought I didn't know you well enough.' We were trying to make character out of what was our problem. We felt that if it was true that we didn't think we knew Denys well enough, maybe what was true of us was also true of Berkeley."

In retrospect, Kurt considered changing some of the dialogue. Originally, it was written for a British accent. "I do think that some of those scenes play a little better with an accent. If I had known that we were not going to do an accent, I would have welcomed the chance to write through some of the dialogue, but that still wouldn't have solved the problem. It would still be a problem of a character that no one understood very well."

I asked Kurt what he would do differently. What can be learned from this situation? What would he tell another writer, facing the same problem?

"I think I would say, on a practical level, be careful of nonfiction, and understand how far you are or are not prepared to go to fictionalize someone. I don't think that there ought to be any rules about that. I have a great regard for the person who says, 'My job isn't history, my job is to deliver the best possible dramatic movie and that is what I'm going to do.' If somebody says, 'What do you think about *Patton?*' I would say, 'I think *Patton* is a mighty fine film, but it doesn't square with my understanding of Patton the man, from reading the history. But it's a great movie and I have no quarrel with it.' But believe me, the next time, if ever I'm involved with a situation where I'm being asked to utilize biographical nonfictional material, I'll be real careful about understanding whether I feel the facts are there and good enough as they are or whether or not I'm going to wind up being disappointed by the truth.

"And, as I think back on this situation, I'd say, 'Some of the problems we licked and some of them we didn't.' "

APPLICATION

When you encounter a character problem, first think through the central concepts in the preceding chapters of this book. If you can pinpoint where the problem is (character isn't consistent, lacks dimensionality, no emotional life, values unclear, etc.), many of the exercises given up to this point can be helpful for breaking through the problem.

If that doesn't work, ask yourself the following questions:

- Have I made my characters specific people, or are they too generalized?
- Do I like them and understand them?
- Are my supporting characters taking over the story? Is this takeover detrimental to the story, or is something interesting developing? Am I willing to follow my characters for a while, just to see what will happen?
- Have I asked "What if" of my characters? Have I tried changing gender? Changing backstory? Changing physicality?
- Am I so overworked that my mind has stopped functioning? Does my life consist only of writing? Have I taken time to experience life, so that I have more to write about?

SUMMARY

Writing good characters is a complicated process. Along the way, it's not unusual to encounter some problems. Getting stuck is a natural part of the process. It happens to even the best of writers. Turning to some of these problem-solving techniques can help ease your frustration, and lead to breakthroughs that can help make your characters work.

Epilogue

The writing of this book has been an adventure. Talking to these accomplished fiction writers has expanded my own awareness of the knowledge and subtle skills it takes to create great characters. Whereas I began each interview with a respect for the writer's work, I ended up with enormous respect for the individual as well. It is obvious from their insights, observations, and eloquence that these were very special people.

So many of the writers emphasized these same points: the importance of observing the life around them and of reflecting on their own experiences in order to better understand their characters. However, what impressed me most of all, perhaps, was that each of these writers seems to have found his or her own inner voice. They all had something of value to say, a certain perspective about life that they communicate through their work. Whether it is about the necessity of breaking down the barriers that separate people, or about redemption, or about people confronting moral choices—there is some individual point of view that threads itself through their writing.

Through my work as a script consultant, I know that writers

can learn to believe in, and nurture, this personal voice. Although talent certainly is an important part of writing, it rarely comes to someone all at once. Talent usually includes hard work, some training, much practice, and learning to believe in and to articulate one's special point of view.

I hope that this book will help to empower you to find your own inner voice and to recognize that your own self-knowledge is a strong beginning point for any character creation. I hope, too, that it will encourage your creative process and in so doing will help to bring your characters to life and make them unforgettable.

Women in Film
Luminas Award Criteria

THE FEMALE CHARACTERS

A. Are multidimensional and are seen in a variety of societal and personal relationships;
B. Reflect the range of age, race, socioeconomic class, physical appearance and occupations present in society at large;
C. Move the story through attitude, behavior, and inner purpose, thereby affecting the outcome;
D. Overcome victimizing circumstances through their own volition; and

THE OVERALL PRODUCTION

E. Provides insight, new awareness, and role models of historical or contemporary women who have made exemplary social contributions;
F. Recognizes the significance to women of issues such as power, money, politics and war, and illustrates the unique perspectives that women contribute to these concerns;

G. Acknowledges the universal significance of issues such as family planning, child care, and equal opportunity employment, and of social problems such as rape, incest and abuse;

H. Demonstrates that sexuality and loving include intimacy, warmth, caring and understanding, and are enjoyed by women of all ages.

Notes

CHAPTER 1

1. Syd Field, *Screenplay* (New York: Dell Publishing, 1979), pp. 31–32.

2. Dick Lochte, "Stardomstruck," *Los Angeles Magazine,* March 1988, p. 53–56.

CHAPTER 2

1. Arthur Conan Doyle, *Sherlock Holmes Selected Stories* (London: Oxford University Press, 1951).

2. G. K. Chesterton, *Father Brown Selected Stories* (London: Oxford World Classics, 1955).

3. Agatha Christie, *Curtain: Poirot's Last Case* (London: Collins/Fontana Press, 1975), p. 7.

4. Agatha Christie, *A Pocketful of Rye* (London: Collins/Fontana Press, 1953), p. 97.

5. Judith Guest, *Ordinary People* (New York: Penguin, 1976), p. 1.

6. William Kelley, *Witness* (New York: Pocket Books, 1985), p. 8.

7. Joseph Campbell, *The Power of Myth* (New York: Doubleday, 1988), pp. 4–5.

CHAPTER 3

1. Lajos Egri, *The Art of Dramatic Writing* (New York: Simon & Schuster, 1960), pp. 36–37.

2. Frank Pierson, "Giving Your Script Rhythm and Tempo," *The Hollywood Scriptwriter*, September 1986, p. 4.

3. Christopher Hampton, *Les Liaisons Dangereuses* (London: Faber and Faber, 1985), pp. 31–32.

4. Judith Guest, *Ordinary People* (New York: Penguin, 1976), p. 83.

CHAPTER 4

1. Ian Fleming, *Octopussy* (New York: New American Library, 1962), p. 13.

CHAPTER 5

1. Art Kleiner, "Master of the Sentimental Sell," *The New York Times Sunday Magazine*, December 14, 1986.

CHAPTER 6

1. Dale Wasserman, *One Flew Over the Cuckoo's Nest* (New York: Samuel French, 1970), pp. 22, 27, 38.

2. Constantin Stanislavski, *Building a Character* (New York: Theatre Arts Books, 1949), p. 25.

CHAPTER 7

1. Moss Hart, *Act One* (New York: Modern Library, 1959), pp. 257–258.

CHAPTER 8

1. Edith Hamilton, *Mythology* (New York: New American Library, 1940), p. 34.

2. Huntley Baldwin, "Green Giant Advertising, What It Is, Why It Is, and How It Got to Where It Is Today," The Leo Burnett Agency, March 1986.

3. For further reading on myth, see Joseph Campbell's *Hero of a Thousand Faces* and *The Power of Myth*; *The Search for the Beloved* by Jean Houston; and Chapter 6 in my first book, *Making a Good Script Great*, which deals with myth in relation to screenplays.

CHAPTER 9

1. Luis Valdez, as quoted in an interview with Claudia Peng, "Latino Writers Form Group to Fight Stereotypes," *The Los Angeles Times Calendar*, August 10, 1989.

2. Statistics from *Window Dressing on the Set*, a report of the United States Commission on Civil Rights, Washington, D.C., 1979, p. 9.

CHAPTER 10

1. Frank Pierson, "Giving Your Script Rhythm and Tempo," *The Hollywood Scriptwriter*, September 1986, p. 4.

Index

INDEX

About the Author

Dr. Linda Seger began her script consulting business in 1983, based on an analysis system she developed for her dissertation on "What makes a script work?" Since then, she has consulted with writers, directors, producers, and companies throughout the world, including Ray Bradbury, Tony Bill, ITC Productions, Beyond Limited, the Sundance Institute, and the New Zealand Film Commission. She has given seminars for ABC, CBS, the staff of Embassy Television and the "MacGyver" series, the American Film Institute, the Directors Guild of America, the Writers Guild of America, the Academy of Television Arts and Sciences, and the Academy of Motion Picture Arts and Sciences, and for producers and writers in Canada, Rome, London, Australia, and New Zealand. Dr. Seger is the author of a previous book, *Making a Good Script Great*. She is married and lives in Venice, California.